ADVANCE PRAISE

"Anne Hand's book is a heartfelt story about the impact of the Holocaust, the strength of the human spirit, and the quest to rediscover her family roots. She shares her loving memory of her grandfather, an immigrant from Vienna, whom she only knew when she was a child but whose fate nevertheless is part of her own identity. She takes us on a journey as she traces the connections to her family's Austrian origins and ultimately regains Austrian citizenship herself.

I've had the incredible privilege of spending 30 years listening to the profoundly moving stories of survivors and their families. Anne Hand's story has touched my heart so deeply, especially when she speaks of the little things, the fragments of the old world that lived on in her family – as in so many other survivor families: Her grandfather's gentle accent, his love of classical music, his Wiener Schnitzel, or when decades after coming to the US he still said, "*Ich komme aus Wien.* [I come from Vienna.]."

Anne is a truly inspiring voice of the third generation, and she beautifully describes the perspective of the grandchildren of survivors. These grandchildren continue to carry the traces of their forebears' history in their hearts, and they know that if their grandparents had not managed to escape, they 'never would have existed, never would have been born.'

Austrian Again is a powerful testament to the deep connection we all have to what we perceive as home, and it's a thoughtful reflection about the experience of exile and dealing with and healing from the wounds of the past." —**Hannah M. Lessing, Managing Director, National Fund of the Republic of Austria for Victims of National Socialism**

"In her exquisite work, Anne Hand invites us to join her on a poignant journey as she seeks to reclaim the Austrian citizenship once held by her grandparents. With gentle prose and heartfelt introspection, she delves into a box of family photographs, letters, and passports, gradually uncovering the untold stories of bigotry and hatred that her Jewish family endured. These were stories her parents and grandparents chose to shield from her.

The book serves as a profound meditation on the memories retained by those who survived the Shoah and the centuries of antisemitism that preceded it. It reflects upon the delicate balance of deciding which of these remembrances to pass to younger generations, as they forge new lives in America. Anne's empowering exploration of what lies beneath the surface of such stories in search of a fuller understanding of her family history, brings her face to face with the deep-seated origins of one of humanity's oldest hatreds and the violence it has continually sparked.

With grace and empathy, Anne underscores the timeless importance of understanding this profound evil — a necessity that remains as pressing for her generation in America as it was for her grandfather Max when he departed from Vienna." —**Fernando M. Reimers, Ford Foundation Professor of the Practice of International Education, Harvard University**

"I loved *Austrian Again*. Taking us along for the ride as she deeply considers the complex meaning of becoming an Austrian citizen, Anne Hand has a way of making the personal feel universal, and the universal feel attainable. It is an engaging and unique ride to be on, an exquisite journey from well-worn paths to trails that Hand is blazing for herself. All stories should draw us in like this, helping us understand that our worlds can be as large as we can envision them, especially when we are confident in who we are and where we come from." —**Jillian Keenan, author of the memoir** *Sex with Shakespeare*

"Anne Hand's heartfelt memoir deftly captures the emotional journey she undertook to bring her family's Austrian Jewish past into the present." —**Lisa D. Silverman, Professor of History and Jewish Studies, University of Wisconsin-Milwaukee, and author of** *Becoming Austrians: Jews and Culture Between the World Wars*

"Austrian Again is a moving personal story that tells the experience of persecuted peoples and the complicated inheritances they leave behind. A beautifully crafted meditation on family legacy, hidden trauma and the promise of America." —**Timothy J. Nelson, Lecturer in Sociology and Public Policy, Princeton University**

"...a fascinating read for anyone interested in Holocaust history, family narratives, or the complexities of identity. It is a heartfelt and beautifully written memoir that invites readers to reflect on their connections to the past and how history continues to shape the present. I cannot recommend it highly enough." —**Readers' Favorite**

AUSTRIAN AGAIN

RECLAIMING A LOST LEGACY

ANNE HAND

ISBN 9789493322998 (ebook)

ISBN 9789493322974 (paperback)

ISBN 9789493322981 (hardcover)

Publisher: Amsterdam Publishers, The Netherlands

info@amsterdampublishers.com

Austrian Again is part of the series *Holocaust Heritage*

Copyright © Anne Hand 2025

Cover image: Christine Van Bree

All Rights Reserved. No part of this publication may be reproduced or transmitted in any form or by any means, electronic or mechanical, including photocopy, recording or any other information storage and retrieval system, without prior permission in writing from the publisher.

CONTENTS

PART I
INTRODUCTION

I. Leaving Home	3
II. A New Life	7
III. Going Back?	10
IV. As a Tourist	13
V. An Unexpected Opening	17

PART II
PAST

VI. As I Thought I Knew It	25
VII. Unpacking the Past	32
VIII. The Warped Frame	40
IX. All in Order	48
X. Letting It Go	53

PART III
PRESENT

XI. The Path Forward	75
XII. Proving the Link	83
XIII. Waiting	101
XIV. Validation	110
XV. Commemoration	118

PART IV
FUTURE

XVI. Connect	135
XVII. Relate	142
XVIII. Shift	148
XIX. Build	153
XX. Be	159

Acknowledgments	167
About the Author	173
Photos	175
Amsterdam Publishers Holocaust Library	181

For the Maxes: past, present and future

"Not everything that is faced can be changed; but nothing can be changed until it is faced." –James Baldwin

PART I
INTRODUCTION

I. LEAVING HOME

I never thought I would write this book. I always thought other people had more interesting stories and lives than I did. I felt my own stable world with its bourgeois problems and center of being had nothing meaningful to offer compared to the elevated traumas and dramas we seek out of curiosity or entertainment – the types of stories that are flashfires as opposed to the slow burns of stability and years blending into each other, marked only by minor blurbs like new traffic lights, repainted crosswalks, or fluctuations of stock portfolios.

I also never thought that my understanding of who I am, where I come from, and where I belong would be so fundamentally altered just by reading the news one morning as I do every day. I never dreamed it would take years of process, discovery, and thought to even scratch the surface of what had been left behind to allow me – that nebulous "future generation" referred to when immigrants state their hopes and dreams – to be able to live out life with an elusively high level of stability and success.

Many of the totemic stories I heard about growing up were centered around my mother's much-loved father. Everyone had kind words about my short, round-faced, sturdy, bald grandfather. He passed away when I was 11, so I have the fond, hazy memories of a child, but from family lore, I am sure adult me would have loved him, too. He was, as people told it, thoughtful and kind yet with a sardonic edge. He was a responsible partner and parent while eschewing responsibility he did not need to take on or no longer served him. He was creative in spaces that were not always welcoming or tolerant of his creativity. He was a businessman whose ventures never quite worked out and a dreamer who was open to the possibilities.

My grandfather, according to the stories, left the home he knew in Vienna as soon as he could, as a 19-year-old, when everything was chaotic: socially, economically, and culturally. With all that unrest and instability, his Jewish background did not serve him well. He had applied for visas to leave and go to Canada or British Palestine as soon as possible. Canada came through first. The life-changing decision was made, and he booked that one-way ticket as soon as possible.

That Vienna of the late 1920s, I had heard and now know in the deepest core of my soul, offered nothing to a working-class Jewish teenager, born on the edges of the Carpathian Mountains into a family of local merchants, who went to trade school for cabinet-making, a career that today is a relic of another time. His siblings had come across the ocean with the undulating waves of immigrants that reshaped New York in the five years between the end of World War I and the United States erecting a barrier of bureaucracy to prevent the waves from crashing onto the shore. Then it was his turn to leave and figure out how to make it work.

He had to come with the blessing of those siblings who needed to support his American visa application. Even with that, it took a while. He left Vienna at 19, but he entered the United States in a roundabout way, through the Niagara Falls border crossing, not Ellis Island, about a year and a half later. In the time it took to get there, at an age when my parents, cousins, brother, and I were cloistered away in college, he bravely sailed to Liverpool and from there to Quebec, went overland to Toronto, and learned English while working and waiting for that last visa. Paying his way, each port was a step closer to reuniting with his older siblings and, after crossing at Niagara Falls, joining their more established New York City lives.

Maybe there was doubt that an American visa really would come through. Maybe there was loneliness. Maybe he questioned what he was doing, if he even should have left Vienna. Maybe, when things were the toughest or most uncertain, he told himself that things hadn't been that bad there, that he should turn around.

As it turned out, and as the next ten years evolved, things ended up being "that bad there" for someone starting their life as a working-class Jew. When we think of that glorious, extravagant, old European culture of the Austro-Hungarian Empire, with castles and ballroom waltzes – grand concerts with full orchestras and salons full of intellectuals – well, that was all gone. Perhaps the decade between the wars was relatively kind to the wealthy or those from more established backgrounds. They are the ones we still read about. They are the Sigmund Freuds or Stefan Zweigs of the world who found their great successes both despite and because of being Jewish during those times.

But my family was not like that. They were not the upper crust, the elite, the factory owners, the literati. Nor were they the ones who converted to Catholicism to enshrine their places in the firmament of the Viennese establishment. They studied trades. They worked in their family-owned shop. They went back to Czechoslovakia for holidays to see their nieces, nephews, and cousins, to catch up on the life they had left behind, and see what had changed, but more importantly, what remained the same.

And yet, despite their lower social status in a place where status deeply mattered, with ever-growing economic and racial storm clouds, some of them stayed. When my grandfather left Vienna, his younger sister was still in school. His mother still ran the family corner liquor store and bar she had officially taken over after his father died. They still lived in the same apartment since arriving in Vienna in 1908 at Klopstockgasse 29 in the Hernals district – still a bit out in the periphery and clearly indicative of their social status but not that far out in today's terms that consider horrific urban sprawl. If he did not want to take a streetcar, no matter the weather, it took an hour to walk to the castle in the city center where he went to trade school. Vienna is easy enough to navigate. It is a comfortable place, even with rumbles of unease and upheaval. Maybe he sometimes felt he should not have left.

Eventually, though, the paperwork did come through and his train entered New York City at Pennsylvania Station. That was the beginning of a new, permanent life. As soon as he could, he proudly became an American citizen, and never looked back. With a few interludes where he lived elsewhere because of military service and work, he lived in New York City for the rest of his life, again in the peripheral outer boroughs. First in the Bronx until he met his wife, then in Brooklyn with his own family, with a last long stretch in South Brooklyn, only a few blocks from Coney Island, its boardwalk, and the vast Atlantic Ocean he had crossed in steerage all those years before.

Sixty-odd years later, when that home close to the water became the only one that stayed constant, my grandfather became the first immigrant I knew. He was my most important immigrant, the one I knew best, the person who first showed me, just by being himself, that the world is made up of all kinds of people, some talking differently or having different habits, tastes, and customs. And that is a wonderful thing.

II. A NEW LIFE

There are a few scattered family photographs and postcards from the ten years after my grandfather crossed those great falls and entered his new life. The ones from the American side of the Atlantic show my grandfather's niece in formal portraiture, looking seriously at the camera, solemn in a new dress. My great-aunt Valerie with friends on the Jersey Shore, walking the boardwalk in stylish '20s beach attire. My grandfather hiking in Westchester County in a jaunty suit, with friends, a pipe in his mouth, and a full head of hair. The ones from the European side of the Atlantic show visits to cousins in Czechoslovakia, with everyone relaxing in their light summer attire. My grandfather's mother conservatively dressed against the spring chill, with the family dog in Viennese streets and parks. My great-aunt Karoline, who they called Karla, in a white-collared shirt, framed as a serious young woman.

Even with global events moving at their inexorable pace in the background, important only in retrospect, even with the multiverse of possibilities narrowing down through an indomitable funnel as a prelude to a way of life and culture being savagely destroyed, life goes on.

Nobody ever talked about those events in the background in a personal way. I knew that those stragglers in Vienna, my great-grandmother and great-aunt, eventually did leave because my mother and aunt grew up with their grandmother and aunts, who lived in an apartment near Central Park with birds as pets and an Old World charm. They still spoke German to each other even if the next generation did not learn it fluently. But that was never an important part of the story I grew up with.

By the time I came along, we were all very American indeed. Straight ahead, no looking back, reciting the Pledge of Allegience, speaking English, continuing to move up as specified by the American Dream. We were the results of the American Dream. Our path was unquestioned. We had two cars in the garage of a house with plenty of space (but no dog since my mother did not want to take care of one along with her children). We went to Disney World a few times. We were registered Republicans and Democrats who voted. We knew that the United States was our home. And we knew that if our forefathers, living and gone, had not come to the United States, we would have been part of the destruction and atrocity during World War II. We never would have existed, never would have been born. We came into being precisely because we were American.

There were some things though – small, cultural things – that my grandfather kept to his last days. Even though he regularly beat my US-born, native English-speaking grandmother at Scrabble, his soft accent stayed. He played classical music exclusively on their record player. He could identify forged antique furniture passed off to museums in 30 seconds flat. He made excellent, precise Wiener schnitzel that was always a treat.

One story – the details of which remain fuzzy to me even though the punchline is crystal clear – stands out. He was with some family members, including my mother or father, at a Bavarian bakery in the Hudson Valley. This was, by far, the best bakery in the region, and they went regularly when in the area. He started speaking in German to the proprietor, a woman about his age who was also an immigrant.

Nobody remembers exactly what the conversation was about. But they do remember when his tone shifted and he narrowed his eyes and looked down his nose at something the woman had said. "*Nein, Ich komme aus Wien* [No, I come from Vienna]," he said to a perceived insult. He came from a real, elevated place. Not from a backward town like that woman did.

Though 50, 60, or 70 years later, after leaving a city and country that had nothing to offer him, after a war that destroyed the little left behind, after rejecting the possibility of return, he was still, definitively, from Vienna.

III. GOING BACK?

The story about coming from Vienna is the one I have heard the most over the years, always getting a good laugh in the car or around the table. But my grandfather had no desire to go back. He built the strong foundations of a life in the United States during a 15-year cross-section of his twenties and thirties. If his story had been a movie, those years would have been relegated to the fast-forward montage, a part of life now referred to as emerging adulthood, when he had to adapt and reinvent himself to a new place and quickly changing times.

As far as I know, he never spoke about that phase of adulthood later on. Finding himself, at his own pace, in a new place, during a time when people were expected to grow up, marry, and procreate more quickly, must have been hard. His personal timeline was more akin to today's. He settled down in his mid-thirties and had children afterward. I can only speculate about the timeline formed, even if they are modern sentiments that I think I can understand. But once set, in limestone if not granite, it was done.

No looking back. No mentioning it years later. Let them all build lives that would be peaceful and prosperous. Lives that would be uninterrupted by the gray clouds that gathered over his early life.

His sisters, on the other hand, did look back. They were also proud Americans, but, in some ways, they kept more of their own, older lives. Sometimes it was out of necessity, and sometimes it was by choice. They never married, living together with their mother. They spoke German to each other, not English. They had some Viennese friends from their childhoods who were now in New York, now American, too. They kept up those relationships and adapted to the pace of their new lives. But they never cut the cultural cord.

I knew they had gone back to Vienna after their mother had passed away, once they retired and had the time, out of nostalgia or curiosity that previously might have instigated intense family debate. They went to the old apartment at Klopstockgasse 29 and their father's grave. I surmise they also went back to other parts of the city long cubbyholed in their memories – schools, parks, and cafes that had once been the centers of their lives. What remained of them anyway.

It had been more than 30 years. Much can change in that amount of time, a full generation after destruction. By all accounts, they had a lovely visit. The remaining neighbors were pleasant and remembered them, the liquor store and bar, and their parents. The neighbors were glad for the successes of how things had ended up, although not venturing into that dark place about why they had to happen half a world away. Going back once, it seemed, was more than enough, even when the sisters kept so much of their older way of doing things.

This is what I know from the stories and vague notions I had grown up with around round-headed and round-bodied people with stubborn blue eyes and capable hands who pushed their way through no matter what. After all, what was the use of overthinking, revisiting ad nauseam things that had been violently stripped away and would never come back? Especially all those years later, knowing they were the lucky ones. Knowing firsthand that life goes on and that they were fortunate enough to be able to build anew in a place that let them work and live in peace. There was no point in dwelling; they had done the best they could with what they had, with love and humor, and support for each other. As the Passover

Seder reminds us of every year, that was more than enough. It had to be.

IV. AS A TOURIST

I had two short and somewhat forgettable experiences that involved Vienna after my grandfather died in 1997.

The first was in 2007. I was out of North America for a while, on one of those short-term working visas that feel like they will last for an eternity when you are used to the cadence of the academic year and measuring life in four-month terms. While in Europe, the land of cheap airfare if you have only a carry-on bag, I visited a friend who was in Budapest for a year. When I realized how close Budapest and Vienna were, I decided to take a day trip. It would have been nice to stay longer, but I had just finished college. I had excitement and exuberance but no savings or promise of savings that come from a real career trajectory. A free place to sleep was the clear, nonnegotiable priority even over a cheap hostel, even if that would have meant extra time in a place that had lived rent-free in my imagination for as long as I could remember. Going for a day would be better than nothing.

My memory of the trip is fuzzy. Three hours in transit, with red upholstered seats and in-carriage carpeting, are all I recall from the train ride. I do not remember anyone taking my ticket or giving me a second glance, unlike a trip to France where I was chastised for not validating my ticket or speaking French. Between Budapest and Vienna, I was like any other North American traipsing around Central Europe who had recently graduated from college and was unsure what to do next and decided to wander around Europe.

I remember the pit in my stomach getting out of the train on that drippy morning, the type of gray winter day that keeps everyone who can stay in bed comfortably ensconced in their blankets. I pulled my green wool winter coat tighter around me and my gray knit cap as far as it would go over my ears, ready to greet the day, whatever it had to offer. There was an urgent pull of wanting to feel something, to connect, when I stepped outside the Central Vienna Train Station on that cold, overcast day during the December slog between Christmas and New Year's. I was not sure, though, what that something was. It could have been anything, but instead, I felt blank.

At first, I was disoriented, so I made my way downtown following a printed map from the tourist kiosk. I recalled from some of the family stories that when my grandfather was learning his trade in high school, the school was in the central castle. With nothing else to orient me, I made my way there first and haphazardly wandered around. I walked through the large, spiked, metal gates and meandered into cold, cavernous, stone rooms that seemed ill-suited for repurposing as classrooms and workshops. It was interesting, but I did not feel anything personally.

It seemed like just another tourist destination. I suppose I could have been more proactive before I went there and asked, for example, about my great-grandfather's grave or if anyone knew anything about my grandfather's life there beyond the vague notion of where he went to high school. But I did not, and maybe I did not want to. Maybe I wanted to get there and feel the electricity that can come from realizing a long-anticipated dream without knowing if it was really a dream.

So I spent the eight hours or so I had in the city meandering around its inner ring, visiting the obvious touristy and institutional buildings and museums – the castle, the cathedral, the opera house. Check,

check, check. A "greatest hits" type of visit, something anyone can easily do on a fire-engine-red double-decker tour bus in most cities these days. I took multiple pauses for the cake and coffee for which Vienna is world-famous to turbocharge my wandering. Then, after it was dark, as it was becoming too cold to enjoy being out in the streets, I got on the train back to Budapest, content enough despite not feeling anything I had thought I wanted to feel. I had been to the Vienna of those stories from so long ago. Wasn't that an amazing thing?

The second experience was about ten years later. I was working for a large international organization and had a colleague whose husband was Austrian. She had lived there beforehand for a few years as well. The three of us went out for dinner to a fancy Indian restaurant in Washington with a pedigree to bolster the cost because the Obamas allegedly liked it. It was not one of the small local mom-and-pop Indian restaurants, usually run by the immigrant generation, I was used to going to with my parents. This was an Indian restaurant befitting people who travel with per diems and expense accounts. I at least had a per diem at the time.

We ate single file at the bar since there were no tables available and we hadn't made a reservation. This was the first time I had spent much time with the colleague's husband, but I had heard about him, and the conversation comfortably flowed. In the middle of the evening, I felt comfortable enough to say "My grandfather grew up in Vienna" openly without thought to the layers that might painfully, immediately, blister back about historical discomfort on both sides of the aisle. At the time, it did not register how messy the situation could have been, what his nationality and upbringing implied about what his grandparents might have done to mine or others. It was not something we thought about; my family had avoided the worst, so it was fine. The rest happened to other people, worlds away.

But he was nonplussed. "It is really a great city," he replied. "You should spend some more time there."

"I should," I said and continued to think as the conversation ebbed and flowed, meandering in a different direction. It would be fun to spend time there, to feel the place differently, and explore the nooks, crannies, and crevices that come with staying in a place for a while and getting to know it. Getting a feel for it that a day or two, or even a week or two, wouldn't even come close to covering. The kind of trip that ends up lasting for several months, without an expiration date in mind, because there doesn't need to be. It might be fascinating to understand where my family fit into such a place, to see if it felt like a kind of home.

But, well, why bother? I did not speak German. I did not have any plans to learn German. I could not work there. I was a type of European by ethnicity but not by nationality, and that meant I could not stay for long. If I wanted to be there longer than a few months, without an expiration date, I would have to get a visa, do lots of cumbersome paperwork, and be there on somebody else's clock. That is, if I was lucky enough to find a job there. The voice in my head said that it was silly. The whole thing would be a temporary exercise in futility.

At that point in my life, I firmly believed that the concept of Americans going back to "rediscover" something about our "roots" that had been warped by memory, never existed, or had completely changed, was silly. Americans, after all, move on and move forward. That is how our country was built. That is the ethos we learn from our families, from school, from the culture all around us. We connect with and relate to that forward motion more than anything else, except for waxing nostalgic for an idealized place that comes from the palimpsest of memory and story. Why bother, indeed? What would be the point of spending more – or as I now realize I thought of it, *significant* – time in a place like that?

V. AN UNEXPECTED OPENING

My outlook changed on an otherwise normal day during the first lull in the coronavirus pandemic during the summer of 2020. In that first phase of working from home, as the world was shut down, I had remotely logged in to a job whose expiration date was drawing nearer after four years. I was experiencing the same low-grade, constant, full-body, unnamable dread and anxiety that I had already been feeling for several months since the pandemic started. In retrospect, I feared the uncertainty of unemployment more than that of getting sick.

The routine in those days was always the same: log on to the computer in my makeshift bedroom office, check email, and start working. I was getting phased out of projects because of my contract end date, so there was not always much to do. When things were slack, I would click through the news, trying to keep busy so I did not have to think about my parents possibly getting sick with this virus that still had no treatments, me being unemployed, or things I could not name but knew would be worse.

One morning, clicking through my normal medley of international news websites, I did a double take when I saw the headline in *The Guardian*: Austria offers citizenship to the descendants of Jews who fled the Nazis. What? I kept up with the news because it was ever-changing: refresh, refresh, refresh. Because it got me out of my head for a few minutes. Because it was what I was supposed to do as a white-collar professional who worked on the edges of current affairs. Even if nobody at work ever talked about what was going on. Nothing in any of these huge international publications applied to me or my life. Was this real?

It was, and Austria would begin accepting applications the next day. None of the other news sites I regularly checked had anything about it, but seeing it on one was enough. I did not know what to think. I did not know what the process was. I did not know what we needed. My grandfather left well before the Holocaust, before formal Austro-fascism, before the Nazis rose to power in neighboring Germany and annexed a willing Austria. He was what we call today an economic migrant before the economic distress turned into something much more sinister. But family stories were floating around whose details I simply did not know. His mother and his sister ... What exactly happened there? They were in New York, they were American, by the time my mother was born, but for how long? When did they get there?

As I mulled over these questions, I vaguely recalled a box my mother had received years before. I was in high school at the time. Old family photos and mementos when her aunt died in California at age 99 as we were the closest relatives. There were passports, I remembered, which we were horrified and slightly fascinated by because they had Nazi stamps. Maybe there were other things, too.

I spoke to American and Canadian friends who had navigated their own descendant citizenship processes. Every country is different, and the rules can change. I had some friends from college, from graduate studies, former colleagues who had become friends, who had navigated this type of process. And I had heard stories over the years. Even with declining populations, Nordic, Anglo, and Germanic countries tend to be rigid about who qualifies as a national if you are foreign-born, if you are multiple generations down, or if people left of their own volition. Many culturally Catholic countries – Ireland, Portugal, Spain, Italy – make it easier, often with the requirement of having one grandparent born there. Austria was notoriously rigid about descendant citizenship, but this was an exceptional pathway it had opened, with an exceptional purpose: righting some of the wrongs of nearly 100 years ago So this was different in so many ways, maybe doable.

I received so much varying advice: "If you can do it, go for it." "It took me four years, but you know how these kinds of bureaucracies are." "I am so glad I did it, it makes the world so much bigger." "If I know anyone who should do something like this, it is you."

Then there was my family itself. My family is small, without extended networks of cousins that so many take for granted. My mother was reticent when I said this was something we both might be eligible for, through my grandfather, or maybe her grandmother. That this was something perhaps we could do together if she wanted. That, if she did not mind, I would probably have to go back into the box that had been sitting unobtrusively under a credenza in her living room for decades. That this was about her side of the family, the aunts and grandmother who had established their own node and lived out their lives in the US on their own terms. She did not say yes, but she did not say no. "See what you can find, then I'll let you know what I think" seemed to be the mode of assent.

Throughout the process, there was a murmuring subtext, which became something spoken aloud once the possibility seemed more real. What would *he* think? What would *they* think? What would *my relatives*, who had left or fled a home that had given them comfort for many years but hadn't served them for a long time and would have killed them had they stayed, think about us giving that place another chance? Was this the legacy they would have wanted? What would my grandfather, the proud Vienna-raised man who never went back, who put it all firmly in the rearview mirror, think? What did it mean for us, as "successful," integrated Americans, to try to take both forks in this path?

The conversation kept coming back to the idea that they, of all people, would understand the importance of having options, of forgiving, of not holding grudges, of moving forward and seeing what the world could offer. We never know what will happen in this unpredictable world. Options are good, and this reconnection to the past seemed like it would be a good one to have. Ironic as it may be, of course, to have the ability to return to a place that so painfully offered some ancestors nothing, and then forced the ones who stayed to flee.

This is the story of going down a rabbit hole from which I have not yet completely emerged and feeling the hole growing, expanding, to encompass both the world and family I was born into, and the world and family I am moving forward into, and still creating for myself. This is the story of discovering things that were not deeply hidden but that nobody had taken the time, reflection, or thought to unearth. This is the story of embracing a bigger world, a world with complications sometimes difficult to reconcile, while knowing that, by trying to live life to its fullest, we are showing it is possible to live with joy today while acknowledging and assimilating the generations-old difficulties that led to this place and time.

To me, for many years, the world beyond what I was familiar with, beyond my daily, weekly, or yearly routine, beyond what I was directly linked to by birth and organic circumstance, was always more exciting. Different, more engaging. More worthy. I now realize my life can seem exotic and interesting to others, and I want to share it more fully. It is hard for me to be the center of attention. I think that is the case for many even if we are smart and capable. By putting myself and this part of my story out in the open, I hope it resonates with others. I hope it allows others to tell their family stories and reckon with how they fit into the world we inhabit and often take for granted.

Before this experience, I never dug deeper into family stories. I took what was told at face value, without questioning why people might be telling these stories. Digging deeper and finding out more felt like committing myself to a burden of expectations. It felt like becoming entrenched in more of that same way of predictable life that did not seem as exciting or interesting as traveling off the beaten path, connecting with people so different from myself, or being thrust into a situation where I had to build the road as I walked on it.

I now realize that perhaps this feeling of movement is natural and normal. I also know that it was shaped by my forefathers navigating their worlds. They knew how to successfully incorporate themselves into them in a way that is more relevant today than ever before.

This whole process would not have been possible without my grandfather, whose chosen name was Max Wald, who was born in a town called Oderfurt that no longer exists in name but does exist in strength and character on the Czech side of a border that has come and gone. He was raised in a Vienna that still exists in name and shape but opens into a different world than the one he and his mother, Irma Wald, and his siblings, Louis, Valerie, and Karla Wald, fled all those years ago. I hope they would be proud of the time and thought that has gone into this book, this existential and spiritual journey of belonging. I hope they would be glad to be remembered like this.

I want to thank them for opening doors for people like me who they never knew would exist and tell them that I am doing my part to ensure they are never forgotten. May their memories, in whatever form they take, always be a blessing.

PART II
PAST

VI. AS I THOUGHT I KNEW IT

There was an initial shock after seeing the news online. I had a strange feeling that I might be able to firmly grasp onto something that had never been real. That is, a connection to a place that had been left behind so long before. Thinking that maybe this was something relevant to me, in a way nothing else I had read in the news had ever been, was jarring. I let it sit for a bit, unsure exactly what to do but the weight of the realization distracted me from focusing on anything else. I reached out to a close friend who had some experience with these types of processes. "Do you have time for a call in the next few weeks?" I asked. He had done Italian paperwork for himself and a few other close relatives. That was different, but maybe enough was the same that he could get me going, at least in terms of righting my head and knowing how to get started.

I told him what I knew just from the little bit of family stories. *My grandfather was born in Czechoslovakia, I think in Bohemia. They moved to Vienna when he was a baby. They stayed there through World War I and he grew up there. Their surname in Austria was Waldapfel. I do not know where his parents were born. I think his father is buried in the main cemetery in Vienna...*

These were the basic outlines of the story. The parts of the story deemed important enough through the years to retell that could take on a life of their own, what people told when feeling nostalgic. A highlights version that was linear enough, or had become so through countless telling and retelling, to make it down to my generation in a way we could understand and keep telling.

As I understood, my grandfather, the third of four children, moved with his family from Czechoslovakia to Vienna when he was a baby. When pressed, he said the family had come from Bohemia, the cultured region around Prague. There was an understanding that extended family had supported this transition and set his parents up running a liquor store and bars to make a living for themselves and their children. His younger sister, the last of the siblings, was born in Vienna a few years later. They were established in what was then the heart of an empire, but he never went into detail about where they lived, or what their house was like, or day-to-day life.

During World War I, my grandfather was in elementary school. The war started when he was six and ended when he was ten. His older, ill-tempered brother had been drafted into the Austro-Hungarian army as a cook. The rest of the family lived in Vienna throughout the war, still running their small corner liquor store and bars. During this extended period with not enough food for not enough people, they traded stocks of liquor from their reserve for enough cabbage so the three children still at home would not be completely malnourished. There was a story about how a neighbor who had gone to the outskirts of the city to scavenge for extra food was shot. All I knew about that time in my family's story was survival and food.

After the war, once things had settled back down, my grandfather went into a trade school program to become a woodworking artisan. He wanted to make musical instruments, which I always found magical in a way, somehow emblematic of the city and culture he came from and that he wanted an active part in maintaining. But there was a guild and his working-class family was not connected to it, so musical instruments were out, and cabinetry it was. His daily commute for years as a teenager was to the majestic city center castle that had been opened for regular municipal use. Back and forth, an hour's walk downtown, or a streetcar ride if he was in a hurry.

Over the years, as he grew up, the family changed. Six people became three. When he was 12, and then again when he was 15, his two older siblings emigrated to the United States. They departed as soon as they were able, never looking back after the end of World War I, before the United States started to put in immigration quotas and restrictions for people fleeing Europe with its messy racial and social tensions. When he was 16, in the mid-1920s, his father, my great grandfather, died of a heart attack. Then he graduated from his cabinetry program and had to figure out what he was going to make of himself.

My grandfather graduated with a skilled trade but no hope of building anything for himself in a cowed Vienna that was a shadow of the vibrant center it had been before the war. There was no work or hope of opportunity for him there. So, in Vienna, the three people that were left in his family became two. As described earlier, he went to Toronto, via Liverpool and Quebec City, upon receiving a Canadian visa. A year later, once his formal American visa sponsorship came through, the 19-year-old crossed over the international bridge at Niagara Falls on his way to join his two older siblings in New York City, his forever home.

That was the story I knew. That was the version I retold on that first call, with a friend who knew for himself the process of rebuilding his own complex identity. He knew firsthand the freedom that came from being able to choose where he wanted to be and when he wanted to be there.

After we chatted, my friend's initial diagnosis was guarded. "This seems doable," he said, without any promises or guarantees. As I was wrapping up my job, he took the time and effort to thoughtfully go onto a few of the genealogy websites that I had previously dismissed as the stuff of hobbyists and cranks who had too much time on their hands. He started with my great-grandparents. I hadn't gone to my parents' house yet and could not for a few weeks to see what might still be around. The internet was the only available place to start.

Before this experience, I had always withdrawn whenever I heard Americans I knew talking about the idea of rediscovering their roots. Going on vacation to a distant place that had once birthed a family member but now was a hundred years removed from that ancestor setting foot in the place seemed a cliché. To me, the stories they told with gusto used the idea of the past to add polish and an extra pastiche of meaning or depth to vacations they simply wanted to take anyway. They wanted to ascribe something extra important to a journey that, as far as I could see, needed none. It seemed like social posturing more than anything else, something artificial, without any real meaningful connection to where they were going.

One image that came to my mind was the prolonged bus-and-pub tours that hedged the Gaeltacht in western Ireland. People were carted around an idealized version of the countryside, likely having had one set of great-grandparents who were from a different part of the country. Or extended family trips to Italy, where everyone stayed at a villa in a location where they may or may not have had roots, and grandmothers came back beaming with Christmas card-perfect pictures.

Now I am a bit ashamed to have thought it was all deluded and hypocritical. After my own journey and discovery, I am not proud of having been so judgmental. We are all looking for something to relate to in this complex world. We want to hang our hats on that connection of meaning. We all do it in different ways.

I mention this judgment on my part only because I don't wish to sugarcoat the preconceptions I brought into the process. Especially since the past was something my own family had clearly left behind, with no love lost, no signposts to guide me toward something more concrete or help me dig more deeply into. Nothing that anybody talked about openly.

My friend got back to me with results from his initial research about my great-grandparents: "Success! Both are Slovakian by modern-day borders. So here is the better detail for your great-grandfather Sigmund Waldapfel: Birthplace is Považská Bystrica, Považská Bystrica District, Trenčín Region, Slovakia. This is still a municipality today. And here is your great-grandmother (née Irma Fischer): Čadca, Čadca District, Žilina Region, Slovakia. Čadca is still a municipality today."

These were places that I had never heard of. Like most American descendants of such places, I could not spell or pronounce them, either. I would not have been able to find them on a map without Google. These were places that were never a part of the story I knew so well that I could recite at a moment's notice if anyone asked (which nobody ever did). They did not involve Prague or Bohemia at all; they were in another country. The story, it seemed, started somewhere else. Somewhere that, for whatever reason, my grandfather did not feel comfortable sharing.

"The synagogue in Čadca was destroyed in 1972. Since that was the place of marriage, that might have been an interesting connection," my friend said.

Interesting indeed. It felt so out there, so far beyond what I was expecting. I was just reading, starting to digest unexpected information, and not sure what to make of something that did not align with any of the specifics that I had understood about my grandfather and what he had shared about who we were.

This new description, borne of databases and archives and an impartial friend who knew how to navigate them well, still felt at arm's length. It felt like I was working through a historical description in an archive, not something personally related to me. I could not, or did not, feel any type of connection. What I did feel was confusion.

"For interest purposes only, if you look up earlier generations (aka grandparents of Sigmund Waldapfel), you will find most of them resided in Topolcany, Slovakia," he said. "Wikipedia includes quite a bit about that city's Jewish history. Just adds to how weird it is now that these cities are ethnically homogeneous after centuries of so much diversity."

So weird. And so weird that I did not know about any of this. Why did I not? And how had it only taken someone a quick keyword search to find something so simple that upended years of what I had taken as unquestionable fact? The whole package was interesting, in a pit-of-my-stomach resignation sort of way. There were real tracks out there, in places I had never heard of, but were part of my story beyond the easy "we're American and Jewish" understanding of identity with which I had grown up.

Even at this early stage, it all seemed hard. It was beyond the idea of Vienna, or even Prague or Bohemia, which at least I was familiar enough with to be able to find on a map. I had no idea why it was something that he wanted to cut off and leave behind. It made me skeptical. If something as simple as this was different than the story I knew, what else was?

It was beyond the artificial simplicity of the mythology we pass on to children, who absorb in unquestioning delight the new stories they hear while comfortable and warm, cozily perched on a grandparent's knee at the dinner table. At this early stage in the process, I somehow already knew that I was going to have to pull myself out of that pastoral memory, pull on my grown-up pants, and do something with whatever came out of this process. It was not a wholly enticing proposition.

In my early years of elementary school, in the extended, semirural, exurbs of the industrial ring surrounding New York City, I remember that once we had to do an exercise on where our families came from. We were given a blank map of the world, and our task was to color in the countries and write their names underneath the map. I was proud and excited because talking to my grandparents, there were lots of countries to color in. I knew Austria because of my grandfather and his accent, but in the middle of the European map there were also Germany, Czechoslovakia, Romania, and Poland. And further east, there were Ukraine and Lithuania, which I remember being confusing and harder to find, especially Lithuania.

It was fun to color in all those countries and see how they skimmed alongside each other but were different, creating a strange and colorful blob with a tiny outlier that I could take to school and say, "Look at all of this. This is me." There was a lot more color, a lot more dynamism and movement, than in the maps of my friends who only had one or two countries colored in.

I loved that map. What nobody is going to begin to talk about with a seven-year-old, though, is that many of these countries in their current blobby forms were new constructs, with new borders, that my family members who lived there and left would probably not recognize. When most of my family members left, these were not countries as we recognize them today. They were either parts of grand empires, loose confederations, or hinterlands on the outskirts of empire.

My family – all Jewish, as far as we know – was part of that sprawling and fragmented people of Central and Eastern Europe. They had their homes and lives in a reality not so different from ours for the most part, at least when things were good. But when things were not good, they were second-class people or worse, undermined and stripped of their opportunities and livelihoods. Once they left, in less than a generation for the most part, what would have felt near and familiar was completely gone.

VII. UNPACKING THE PAST

My parents still live in the townhouse-style condominium with blue-gray siding where I spent the second half of my childhood. The condos were originally summer cabins, then were converted into year-round living when 25 miles from Boston was not just the country anymore. It is where I say I grew up when people ask.

I know all the possible ways there from any spoke within a ten-mile radius. The winding roads in the northwest suburbs that for centuries were primarily for farmers to bring their crops to market now go past a mix of commuter housing, conservation land, and commercial necessities for the residents. When we moved there, there were still quite a few local farms. Now I can count the ones remaining on a few fingers, and most have been intentionally preserved to keep something alive of the character of what the town used to be. There is no reliable public transportation even though there really should be – distances to run errands are too far to walk and the roads are too dangerous to bike because of all the cars.

I prefer to think of the area by its geographic features because they do not change even though the lightly undulating farmland has made way for strip malls and tract housing and many swamps have been filled in. There are the interconnected back roads, the walking and hiking trails that aren't clearly marked, the reserves named for local donors and local martyrs whose names would not register for anyone outside of this radius, the pond in front of the turnoff from the busy local thoroughfare to my parents' development. The pond is actually a reservoir, which was the subject of a not-so-friendly water-rights dispute between neighboring towns for decades. Because it is a reservoir, no trail traces its shoreline, and there are no plans to build one even though it would be nice.

The conserved woods and wetlands have remained the same, with their regular seasonal changes, in the quarter century since we arrived. Many things, too, are the same inside the condominium: the layout, the living spaces, much of the furniture. Our bedrooms are fixed, although we have all grown and aged, but they are there as a concrete, stable representation of home no matter what I may do or where I go. Over the years, I have updated the small rectangle that has been my space since I was in elementary school, but the more communal spaces remain as I remember them through my late childhood, with old photo albums tucked into bookcases and scattered art, memorabilia, and mementos left undisturbed in the same spots for decades.

The nondescript, unlabeled cardboard banker box that I asked if I could go through was among the items. It had lain dormant for 20 years, sitting under the straw-colored Norwegian teak credenza that housed a hodgepodge of holiday-specific platters, special-occasion stemware, and odds and ends that had also ended up behind glass. I felt it had been well placed as I dislodged it. The box was unobtrusive, yet almost everything I needed ultimately ended up being there for the taking, hiding in plain sight.

My mother received the box when I was in high school after my grandfather's older sister passed away in San Diego just shy of her 100th birthday. I remember the surprise at receiving it as well as initially feeling overwhelmed. My mother probably went through it in depth at the time, but I did not. When we first opened it up back in 2002 or 2003, I got as far as the old-fashioned, paper Austrian passports toward the top of the box. I remember paging through them, noting the retro photos and spindly handwriting, then stopping suddenly as I got to the pages with swastikas stamped on them. My mother put them each in small plastic sandwich bags, and back into the box they went.

When I first reopened the box on that mid-October afternoon, for the first time in who knows how many years, there was a hodgepodge of over 100 years of ... well, stuff. It all seemed random, as though my great-aunt Valerie's desk drawers had been emptied without a care and their contents swept into the box regardless of import or significance, as though the executor had thrown together discrete piles of "personal artifacts" and shipped them off. There were photographs from Europe, the United States, and Israel that appeared to span 100 years, from the late 1800s until the birth of my brother and me toward the end of the 20th century. There were postcards from the 1930s and calendars from the 1970s. Address books with street names and phone numbers crossed out and updated as people moved around over the years. There were documents, some thrown in and others neatly tucked away in envelopes. All of it was mixed and mismatched in a way I could not grasp. I never knew that one small box could feel so chaotic. Considering that everything had been tossed in and shipped across the country, with no attention paid to the conservation of anything or a basic "what if the box got wet," it was amazing to see the relatively good condition everything was in.

Amid the stuff, there were clear reminders of their lives in Europe a lifetime ago. There were letters – both typed and handwritten in fancy and fancier German script – and posed pictures of the kind I had mostly seen in museums and must have been a luxury item. There were birth and death announcements in German with Hebrew block print complementing. And pictures, mostly of people. So many pictures. Too many pictures. Most importantly for my initial purposes, there they were, easy enough to find – the two Austrian passports I had vaguely recalled, still in their 20-year-old plastic sandwich baggies.

I do not know why the box came to us rather than another member of my mother's generation, but maybe it had to do with me. The first thing I distinctly recognized, sorting through everything, was my own painstaking handwriting, in short letters on my mother's stationery, and postcards from local Hudson Valley landmarks, sent when I was four, five, six years old. In this digital age, I still love to send physical mail, especially postcards – a lifelong training and habit that stuck. I wonder if those reams of childishly formed letters tipped the odds of receiving this small piece of history in our favor. I wonder if Aunt Valerie, whom I only met in person as a baby, somehow cosmically knew this would be the right place for all the material, that it would somehow find both a practical and transcendental use.

Initially, I tried to address the box's contents with the detached precision of a surgeon. It already seemed like it might be a lot to jump in fast and feel the emotional involvement of diving in the deep end headfirst. I could not let myself feel that so early in the process when I was beginning to put everything together. I mechanically rifled through all the different textures of paper: from the smooth, shiny matte that photographs were printed on, to the rough folds of letters, to the durable heft of passports, looking at them but not seeing, just feeling in a purely tactile sense. I tried to keep everything clean. I tried not to let the box and its contents pull me in … or under.

As much as I tried to approach my task calmly, I quickly realized it would be impossible. Although there was only one box and it wasn't that big, it felt like a bottomless pit. Starting to register everything felt like I had unintentionally fallen into a vast well I would have to claw my way out of. The passports were there, floating on the surface, easily skimmed off. But not so far below, I could see the swirling, unwieldy, confusing mass in its own little vortex, and I could feel myself tipping in, all the way, despite part of me trying to pull back and keep my feet on the ground.

But I could not resist this force. Something in me needed to jump in headfirst without pause or reservation and feel whatever I would feel. I could not control it. It was the same feeling that afterward forced me to write about it. It was an uncontrollable urge that I still cannot understand as someone who's spent most of my life trying to contain feelings, fit in, and not visibly be too much even if I felt big things inside. These feelings about the box and whatever happened with its contents were overwhelming. I could not let go or let someone else discover what was inside. I knew I had to do it myself.

My initial sorting process was separating things and people I recognized from those I could not. There were baby and childhood pictures of me, my brother, my first cousins, my mother, my aunt, my mother's first cousin. There were my grandparents at much younger stages than I had known them. I recognized my grandfather, so young, with dark curly hair, a pipe between his teeth for a jaunty effect, and older, bald, his weight yo-yo-ing between solid and stout, but still much younger than I had ever known him. There were those I quickly recognized as my great-aunts Valerie and Karla and my great-grandmother Irma. There was an original of the only full family portrait I had seen elsewhere of my grandfather's nuclear family, taken when he was about seven years old.

In particular, the pictures of Valerie and Karla made me smile. There they were, individually, younger versions of themselves in the 1920s and 1930s, separated by an ocean. And there they were again, together, living their best lives, retired in the 1970s, two round older ladies traveling together, relaxing together, the family resemblance completely undeniable. There was also documentation of their intertwined lives – of gravesites bought and fully paid for together at Mount Moriah Cemetery, just over the Hudson River from Manhattan. There were old agendas from 1975, 1983, and other years when it seemed like nothing important had happened; why on Earth did anyone commemorate those trips around the sun?

There were also many people and things I did not recognize as I worked backward through the generations. It helped that many photos and postcards were labeled or dated, but most were not. At least those with years let me put things in some type of order. Some of the photos and postcards were ripped or split, and I had to search to see if the other parts were still in the box. Some had the same people, the same groups. There were several photographs of the same man I had never seen before in a period bathing suit that was bunched in odd places. There were postcards, nearly 100 years old, with Czechoslovakian stamps, posted from towns I had never heard of and could barely attempt to pronounce. There was a scrap of paper with a name and an address, the same name that appeared on the back of two photographs of the same boy, first with his father, then as a teenager. And so much more.

The late autumn Massachusetts sun became fainter as the afternoons passed, turning to winter. I could accomplish little in the outside world as a pandemic with no end in sight made all in-person activities feel like a leap of faith, so I began to organize, spreading out the material across a small quadrant of the old living room carpet. First, I made separate piles. The things I recognized, the copies of photographs I had seen in our photo albums or my grandparents', were easy and went in one pile. There were some small booklets with dates. Transatlantic crossings from 1923, 1938. The passports, of course, but only from 1938. Letters, some dated, some not, mostly from 1938. An old Morocco leather accordion file, just the right size for a passport or two. Some original documents on legal-sized paper, some certified copies, all in German.

And so many photographs, black and white, then color, of people I did not know. I separated the story I knew from the one I did not, the color from the black and white, like it was the *Wizard of Oz*. In color, there was life I recognized and a flow. I saw my great-grandmother, wrapped in blankets, smiling dreamily, lounging in the same muted northeast American winter sun. I saw my great-aunts on their retirement world tours and recognized Jerusalem and Yaffo, where I had also been once, as well as their home at the time in California, with friends. There was a photo of my great-grandfather's grave in color, which they must have taken on that trip to Vienna, and odds and ends that were thrown in the box for reasons I cannot decipher. And multiple photographs from the 1930s of a dog named Petey.

Sifting through the box was a weighty task even without being able to read the letters written during the interesting times that had cursed them. I started and stopped, piled and re-piled, taking things in and out, unsure how to proceed. I let it sit for a day, a few days, a week, then came back to it, drawn like a moth to the flame for reasons I could not say but that left a gnawing uncertainty. I took pictures of the letters because they were too delicate to put through the one-page-at-a-time travel scanner I had available. The old photos were sturdier and I scanned some of them. I tried to create, order, divide without becoming too rigid in my categorization because I did not know if my excavations were uncovering a new species or just an extension of something I already knew about. I went in circles in my head about everything inside the box.

What could it mean, this box that opened up worlds that I had no idea existed? I had no context for much of its contents. I had the broad-strokes narrative of more immediate family who were present and accounted for, but there were so many more people whose faces shone with hope and life and were completely unknown to me. Most of those faces seemed unrelated to the well-trodden stories I knew.

Despite being a fully formed product of ten years of twice-weekly religious and cultural Jewish education, despite having what I thought was a solid background in my past, I realized something that startled me. I knew what happened during World War II and after. However, I realized that I did not know much about the time just before it when these people would have been living their lives. I had no idea what they would have engaged with, how they would have felt about things, or what their normal lives would have been like. Lives they never willingly left behind, with some dying in the process of trying to hang on.

I knew a story about American immigration and what happened on this side of the Atlantic. I was exposed to it as nostalgia that becomes its own religious education and mythology. It was a part of acceptable entertainment: an American tale, hearing about girls working their way up and out of sweatshops on the Lower East Side, triumphing over adversity. Things like that. Up, over and out, toward the American Dream.

No one explored or explicitly addressed tropes about European life on their own merits or terms. It was always glossed over, seen as a precursor to the inevitability of the Holocaust, to the camps and summary executions, in a linear version of the story. With nobody wanting to explain to me as a child why or how countries can change borders, be born, reborn, and ever mutable, nobody wanted to explain the kaleidoscope of Jewish life that existed in all its complexity either. I didn't know about Jewish life in its different forms amid these changes that nobody could control while hoping for the best outcomes. *Fiddler on the Roof* was assumed to be representative. As a child, I had never heard of Isaac Bashevis Singer or Stefan Zweig, let alone read them, or understood what they were trying to memorialize about the complexity of these worlds so far gone.

VIII. THE WARPED FRAME

For weeks, I could only guess who most of the people in the unnamed European pictures were as I sorted and re-sorted off and on while making up stories in my head. These photographs were a bit different, more tricky, much less contextualized. I tried to find patterns and meaning in people, locations, clothing. I shuffled through clear differences, trying different strategies to create some order. Could I see the same people aging over time? Were the people on ships crossing the Atlantic all aboard the same one? Were they different ships that just looked the same? What about the parks, the beaches, the boardwalk? I spread tentatively separated piles on the old carpet, seeing if the answer I thought I was looking for held. Most of the time, it did not, and I re-sorted – back to square one.

Some of the European images were so casual and comfortable: summer pastorals whose innocence belied the destruction to come. A peace that would be shattered in only a few years. The two little boys with their ears sticking out, shriek-laughing and playing, with a row of other children out of focus behind them. A dozen teenagers holding a couple of lambs and a bouquet of flowers dressed up for a fancy day in the countryside. A serious, intense young man with thick hair and brows and an uncompromising gaze into the camera, formally framed and captured, commemorated at that moment.

Three of the photos were personal photographs printed out as postcards, which enchanted me. Two seemed to be the typical postcards that you'd buy to commemorate a visit somewhere, although only one, sent from the town of Rajec to New York City, was a bucolic site, an Alpine-style house centered off a road with a craggy peak behind it. The other was an industrial landscape – smokestacks and railcars aplenty, likely processing the coal that Ostrava, where my grandfather was born and where his mother still had family, was known for at the time. It was sent to Vienna with a short note that I could not fully read, but what I could understand led me to think it was my great-grandmother writing to her daughter, saying she'd arrived.

The other postcard I found adorable and so clever. It was three children – two girls and a boy, aged approximately six, eight, and nine, the girls proudly smiling at the camera in their summer dresses, the boy warily gazing but still directly engaged. They wore clothes that any child today also would except for the socks and shoes that, I imagine, would be replaced by some type of sandal to better enable orthopedically sound scavenging in the heat. It seemed to be a picture printed as a postcard to send to family near and far. That was the one I wanted to read, to understand which cousins or nieces or nephews these children were. To find out the connection. To understand what had happened to them.

Hans and Ernst Fischer were the only names in all of those European pictures that were grounded. Those names allowed me to dig a little deeper. They were a detour, a sidebar from the broader research of getting to the goal of successfully becoming Austrian, again. But they seemed important even if I did not know why. My great-grandmother's family name was Fischer, so I imagined Ernst and Hans, the father and son, were a nephew and great-nephew pair. Ernst looked about the age of my grandfather's older brother. Ernst and Hans were the first two names I had from anywhere, anytime, of extended family concretely. These were real people, and there was a whole life back there, back then.

Hans was in two photos, and maybe the boy in the postcard was also him, but I could not say with certainty. I knew the other photographs were of him because "Hans" was written on the back and there was also a piece of paper with his block-printed full name and address, which had been saved for some reason. There was no other Hans mentioned elsewhere. Hans was there, as a boy in 1930, curled up with his father, Ernst. Then he was there again, alone, older, in 1935. Resplendent in a perfectly tailored bespoke suit, he posed in a photography studio, as a mini adult, not quite fully mature but far enough along to know what type of respectability he would need to project in the future.

I took some of the new skills I was developing and went through online databases, Holocaust archives, and targeted Google searches. So many resources were out there hiding in plain sight, so incredibly useful if you had the need. It is unexpectedly easy now, with just a tiny bit of information, to find some of these people if they happened to be noted on a list or in a database. Indexing or machine learning have made those troves of archives available with the tap of some keys and the click of a mouse from anywhere in the world. If people do not access them, it is because they do not know they exist, do not have a name and place to start with, or do not want to know what happened.

I went fully down Ernst and Hans's rabbit hole. It took me a few days and a couple of dead ends, but I found them without much trouble. They were memorialized with just enough extra context to make it clear that their lives were undoubtedly brutally interrupted in a way that I had never understood as something that happened to my own family.

What I discovered was that Ernst Fischer was involved in local politics. The Jews of Ostrava had obtained 60 seats in the town council in 1921, including representatives from the Jewish Democrats, the Zionist Party, Jewish Laborers, and Jewish Czechs. In 1931, the first

Jewish Party conference was held in Ostrava, and in 1935, he was elected as the party's representative in the Senate. In the same year that Hans posed proudly in his new suit, his father was elected to Czechoslovakian political office.

Ernst would have been an obvious local target when, a few years later, after annexing Austria, the Nazis came into Czechoslovakia and began extending their persecution program to Moravia. But his trail went completely cold after that. Much as I searched the databases, typing in the same name with slightly different parameters or keywords, thinking that the filters would make a huge difference, much as I tried to find more in the archives about what happened to the Jews of Ostrava, I could not locate anything. I could not find anything about Ernst being deported or killed, but local Jewish politicians and leaders were among the first to go. I could only assume he disappeared in the way that countless opposition politicians disappear in fascist or wartime regimes.

I did find Hans in online databases. After I found the details of his ultimate story and fate, there was no unseeing it. After I saw it, I think I would have preferred not to know what happened. But I knew, and there was no way to unknow after that. Shortly after Poland was invaded, in the autumn of 1939, Hans was deported from the only home he ever knew, forced to go the ten miles and then a million worlds away across the Polish border to the pilot version of what became the concentration camps and death camps.

I had never heard of this camp, Nisko. But I looked it up and quickly learned that it was the first stab at creating what became the network of death camps that dotted southern Poland. If you're looking at all of this in a more abstract, technocratic kind of way, I suppose it made sense logistically to first deport the people furthest from the core, who lived closest to the border, and begin to test drive these routes and camps. That is the kind of sense that a bureaucratic middle manager obsessed with pilot programs to ensure process efficiencies would be very happy with.

What that meant, in practical terms, was that my great-grandmother's beloved nephew and close cousin to my grandfather – my own family member – was carted across the Polish border when he was 17 in the first regional shipment of Nazi-determined undesirables and disappeared from any records after that. I found this laid out in stark black and white in databases available from both Yad Vashem, the Israeli Holocaust memorial in Jerusalem, and the US Holocaust Memorial Museum in Washington. There he was, on the train transport documents. And then nothing more. Nothing in the online databases, nothing on Google. At least nothing that I could find. He had gone from the well-heeled son of a local politician to disappeared in less than five years, before he was an adult.

Without knowing exactly what happened to Hans, the hopeful, romantic part of me wants him to have escaped the camp, run into the forest, become the type of resistance fighter that held on tooth and nail, helped people, and survived the war. I want him to have fought for those six years until he was 23, changed his name, and moved on, likely to Israel, where he would have had a chance to rebuild his life and create the type of world he wanted to live in. I want him to have been able to live his life as though he was born when I was, as though the fascism and war that killed so many people had not happened. But I look at that dapper boy in that suit and the realistic part of me doesn't think that is likely to have happened.

What do I think happened? I think that when he was forced onto that train, at the barrel of a gun, on that nippy October day and not allowed to go anywhere else, his father had probably already disappeared. I think he was shocked and confused. I do not think anyone told him where he was going. I think that, even if he packed warm clothes, they were probably taken from him early in the trip. As much as I want to be hopeful, I think that he was cold and malnourished, and got sick and died, during that first winter when he was thrust, behind the barrel of a gun, into the cold and dark belly of hatred.

It was cold and dark where I was, too, and only getting colder and darker. Some afternoons, around two or three, at the warmest part of the day, looking out my window at the line of bare birches and perennial pines, I had to force myself to go out, take a walk, get moving, even for just half an hour. If I did not, it would be another day fully enveloped in my stillness, thinking for hours about this world so far gone, where I did not leave the house, did not get any exercise, just sat at a screen and let the world go by. It did not feel so bad to let the world go by those days, as crusted over with gray grimness as everything seemed to be.

Yet even as news reports showed coronavirus exploding exponentially and the death count beginning to peak, I felt grateful in a way to be stuck in my own little cave. Even if I could not leave very much, I was warm and safe, we had food, and we saw as few people as possible. We were all fine. Hans was not fine during that first winter and would never be fine again. My own isolation, the pandemic, and what I had to do to survive seemed trivial compared to the experiences I was uncovering, which could have been me in another place and time. It allowed me to keep going, keep working. Whatever I was experiencing, as upsetting and disturbing as it was, was not as bad, and at least I could take some measures to mitigate my own fate.

Hans was deported, forced to leave the only home he had ever known, in October, and the winter would have been long and cold. Hans likely did not live very long after he got on that train. And I think that must be why his photos were in the box.

Whether or not they knew exactly what had happened to Hans, I am sure that my great-grandmother and great-aunts knew it was not good. And they knew it was not fair, it was not right, and he was loved in the brief time he had on Earth. They did not want him to be forgotten even if they did not know what fate had befallen him. He, like many others, had the bad luck of being born Jewish in Czechoslovakia, right across the border from Poland, being alive when the Nazis came to power and not having a way out.

Once I realized what fate had most likely befallen Hans, I did not want to find out any more stories. The details of what happened to the happy youth group with some lambs in photos from the countryside, for example, are not what matters. Because of where they were from, if they did not get out in time and go to England, the Americas, Asia, or anywhere beyond the grasp of what eventually became occupied by a tyrannically antisemitic force, the most likely result was that they died. That was it. That was the reality.

When I was young, in Hebrew school, and some people talked about those still alive in their immediate families who had survived the war and the camps – or discussed whatever was highlighted to brand into our impressionable minds "There but for the grace of G-d go I" and "Never again" – I always felt lucky to not have such stories. Nobody in my family would have ever been on "Schindler's List" or collateral damage within "Europa Europa," both of which we watched many times in class. All my grandparents were alive, and they were all American. Nobody in our family was murdered. We were American. We were safe. But now, beyond a reasonable doubt, I knew that was not and had never been the case, and the comfortable thought that I was not personally engaged with this type of death on a grand scale was wrong. I could trace only one story, but there must have been many more.

It was a lie. Maybe a lie with benevolent intentions, to allow the past to roll by and not sully the present and the future, but it was still a lie. Countless family members were murdered. We just did not know anymore in most cases who they were, how they were related, and what the connection might have been to the here and now. And now, three generations later, so much time had passed that the only way to start to sift through the clues of this morbid, digitally enhanced scavenger hunt was through scraps of paper and notes jotted onto saved pictures. And all of this, even in the best-case scenario, would never fully stitch everything back together.

I was not going to, I could not, go down this firebombed path of destruction, desperation, and despair. It was too much, too horrifying, too personal, too bleak. What I could do was focus on the now – the puzzle of life that did still exist, and what actions people take without consciously thinking they are walking a line between life and death.

I could explore their worlds in a way I had never thought to, had never wanted to, with more empathy and understanding than many others could muster or than I could have mustered before. I could take all of this and, with or without some approved paperwork from Austria, push myself to do better. To speak up for the people who might now be my great-grandparents and their families and who might, three generations down the line, have success and well-being far beyond mere hopes of survival.

IX. ALL IN ORDER

Irma and Karoline Waldapfel, my great-grandmother and great-aunt, did make it out. We all knew this since my mother had grown up going to visit her grandmother and aunts in their beautiful rent-controlled apartment around the corner from Carnegie Hall in Midtown Manhattan. By the 1950s, they had established their own little node and lived comfortably in it, guided by the firm hand of my great-aunt Valerie, who left Vienna at age 19 in 1923 and was the driver behind their flight in 1938.

But when I started to dig, nobody still alive seemed to know what had happened in much detail. They got out after the Anschluss, when the Nazi regime annexed a willing Austrian state, and were lucky. My great-grandmother had one business left, a corner liquor store and bar, and she had to sell it. What they got from the store was not much, barely enough to cover their passage to the United States, but it got them out. They became American citizens as soon as they possibly could. These descriptions were sketches, ideas, motifs, more of a vague impression rather than the full painting developed in living color.

What the box had, scattered among the photographs, was a series of letters that viscerally shocked me after I fully understood what they were. Twenty years earlier, we had registered the passports as important, but the letters had somehow escaped notice even though the gnarly, old-fashioned handwriting and the odd size of the sheets of paper made them stand out. There were seven letters; five were handwritten and two were typed. And the first thing I understood, with my limited German language skills, were the dates. They were from December 1937 to May 1938, which stopped me cold in my tracks and sent a wave of chills down my spine.

It was difficult for us to decipher them even at a high, conceptual level. The handwriting was faded and difficult even for a native German speaker to read. Initially, I sent photographs of them to a friend in Germany, who then sent the files to his parents, not asking for translations, which are so much work, but just to know if they said anything about the political circumstances, the big picture enveloping them, and how they felt about it. However, there was nothing in the letters that reflected the coming storm, nothing deeply philosophical that showed premonitions of the looming catastrophe. Sometimes there were high-level details, but then there was family life, gossip, and what they were eating for dinner on the day they happened to be writing. Nothing that would necessarily indicate they had premonitions or knew that things would fall apart so quickly. My friend's father added something I did not know – that people self-censored, unsure who might intercept their letters, so they quite likely hid their full range of emotions and feelings. Fine, fair enough. I let it go at that point, organized them by date, put them in a file folder, and closed the box again.

On a second pass months later with the curators at the US Holocaust Memorial Museum, as we were preparing to donate the full set of letters, we got initial summaries in English. The summaries, with the other pieces of what I had heard over the years, were enough to color in a story that finally made sense about what happened. I realized why they were able to get out when they did, so quickly, as though by a miracle. The type of miracle that makes its way into holiday stories – the miracle of the lights lasting at Hanukkah or the miracle of sparing the first-born sons at Passover.

The miracle, it seemed, was over a decade in the making. Sometimes we make our own luck, laying the groundwork so that it mitigates awful things we never could have expected or anticipated. From the family stories, I knew that my grandfather and his siblings in New York had wanted their mother and youngest sister to emigrate from Austria for years, and join them. For those building a life for themselves in the New World, there was no love lost between this entirely new place with the lives they were building, and the place they left behind that had limited what those lives could be. But their sister did not want to leave, and their mother did not want to leave her behind. It stayed in that stalemate for many years, across an ocean, neither side budging from their desire to uproot.

Then something changed, and I do not know what. Maybe things got bad enough in Nazi Germany, with the Austrian Fatherland Front more and more sympathetic to the Nazi cause, that the letters from New York became more urgent, more pointed, intimating more dire consequences. Maybe the changes that the Austro-fascist government directly made were beginning to become intolerable – elevating Austrian Catholicism at the expense of what remained of Hapsburg-era religious tolerance and diversity, crippling the already weak economy even further under the guise of austerity politics, indulging Nazi-led terrorist attacks. Maybe as all of these smaller pieces began to cling together, become tolerated, create larger patterns, the worry from Vienna became more palpable. Maybe slowly, reluctantly, the pleas from New York started to make more sense and they started to make plans.

Whatever the tipping point, whatever the straw that broke the camel's back, that inflection and change of direction is lost to us now. Which, knowing my family and how we communicate, is not a huge surprise. We are not ones to share our pains when things are not going well. We are more inclined to avoid those uncomfortable conversations and push things aside in the hopes they will resolve on their own. To this day, difficult conversations do not happen, and what is communicated tends to have a positive spin rather than a more radical honesty or transparency that would allow for a more direct reckoning with what is or has happened.

Nobody in my family talked to the younger generations about when a decision was made, and there were no clues in the letters, either. The letters started once a decision had already been made, however it was made, whoever made it. The letters started once it was hopefully only a matter of time until the paperwork came through.

In the letters, Irma and Karoline lived through their last Viennese winter writing to New York about cauliflower soup, the cold, family matters, and other normal goings-on. They worried that despite family support, it would be difficult to get visas to the United States, but they finally went to fill out their visa applications in early March 1938. My great-grandmother fretted about whether she could still call herself a businesswoman on the paperwork since they were not making much money and depended on remittances from New York. But she did anyway.

Only a few days after filling out those forms, after the Reich subsumed Austria, everything about processing their visas accelerated at a miraculous rate that would never happen today, even in similarly dire circumstances. Even though they had only submitted their visa applications a few weeks before, they had appointments at what had formerly been the American Embassy in Vienna (downgraded to a consulate since the new capital was Berlin) for interviews and physical examinations in mid-April 1938. The Americans had to bring in a translator during the interviews since Irma and Karoline spoke no English, but everything seemed fine. They were conditionally approved in late May, pending their procurement of passports and exit visas, and had the help of friends and neighbors to organize everything and get out as soon as possible.

They left Vienna three weeks later, on Sunday, June 12, 1938, with their passports issued and transit visas for Switzerland and France stamped in and resident visas for the United States approved and in the formal quota registry. The passports included customs and police checks from the newly installed Nazi authorities. They were valid for only two years. Use it or lose it.

They used it. They traveled by train, crossing the Alps until they gracefully descended into northern France and reached the coast. Once in Cherbourg, they waited for the ship that took them to New York, where they arrived on Monday, June 20. They were processed at Ellis Island like so many tired, poor immigrants before them yearning to breathe free. Then was a short ferry ride to family waiting in the harbor. To journey further uptown probably required a taxi since they had all their luggage with them, meaning the subway was not a viable option, especially for a woman in her sixties after a long trip. The journey ended in a small apartment one block away from that most American ballpark, Yankee Stadium, in the Bronx, where my grandfather, his sisters, and his mother would all live together again.

After that, they must have crashed. I cannot think of anything else reasonably that could have happened after so many months of heightened uncertainty when they knew the stakes were high but not how high they actually were. There were no longer any close or loving ties to the city and country they had called home for a generation, where they had already survived a war and lived with the slow drip, drip, drop of disintegration, of loved ones leaving for lack of a reason to stay. They were gone, they were out, and they were safe.

X. LETTING IT GO

Once in New York City, my great-grandmother and great-aunt started to adapt. They learned English as quickly as they could and settled in, safe from the destruction that would soon ravage everything they had left behind. As far as I can tell, none of their extended family in Czechoslovakia survived. I know of no cousins who came to visit later, no word from Israel, nothing to indicate that those they loved a devastated world away made it through. And maybe that's why there was no looking back, even for an instant. By the time my mother was old enough to remember, nearly 20 years later, nobody discussed any of it, at least not with the kids around, at least not in the language, English, that the children could understand. When those children became adults and had children of their own, nobody thought to bring it up or ask while that older generation was still alive. It just was not part of the conversation.

This approach seems to have been common, from other people I have talked with whose families fled Germany and Austria during this period – when things were getting worse but before they became devastatingly fatal with no way out. While I know there is a deep literature on shorter-term trauma for recent groups of immigrants and refugees and their immediate families, for a few particular reasons, I was curious about the people in this group – my group – those of us related to yet far removed from the actual atrocities and traumas.

One reason is that I was not sure how much other people in these types of situations knew. In my family's case, of course, we knew little before I started digging. The people who directly experienced these world-shattering events in one way or another have all passed away, and since nobody ever talked about it, there is nobody to ask anymore. I pieced together everything about their flight from records and letters, but if those letters had not been saved, I am sure everything about that last stage of their life in Vienna would have been lost as well.

Maybe other people knew more. That wasn't the case with my family. Our history was dust in the wind, and I was pretty sure I had found everything I could. I wondered, though, if other families who had experienced these events from their own vantage points had been more open with each other and the younger generations. Maybe the stories that other people heard passed down from their parents and grandparents were more open and clearer about what they did and why they did it.

Another reason was assimilation. Today, we know that we are American and, as far as I could tell, my family members have considered themselves thoroughly American as long as they have been on these shores. They deeply believed in the fundamental power of individualism and organized capitalism that, according to what is taught in school, has allowed the United States to become the massive economic force it is today. They believed in the power of hard work being enough to pull themselves up, and that was how they lived their lives. They believed in the American Dream, if you will, in its purest form, back when it was more attainable.

Learning more about the lives of my relatives in early 1900s Austria made me realize that my family had also assimilated back in their original homeland. Maybe that made leaving Vienna and adapting to the United States easier. When they lived in Vienna, their district was a hub of recent migrants to the city from all walks of life. Vienna was the center of a multicultural empire, with its own diverse rhythm and flow, until the empire fell apart. And before that, they had lived at the edge of what's now a tri-border nexus, and they regularly conducted their business in five or six languages. They were used to living in different places, with different kinds of people. They adjusted, they adapted, they made it work, and they always had.

The last, and maybe most sensitive reason, was a question about what victimhood meant to people who had suffered through these experiences. Before digging and finding out these pieces of family stories, I hadn't ever considered my family to be Nazi victims, at least not in the way you read about it in the history books. The way I was brought up, the way I learned about what had happened, the victims were the ones who were killed, who were sent to camps and ghettos. They were the ones who died of violence, neglect, and disease. They lost everything and never recovered, never built things back up as quickly or easily because they could not. Everything had been destroyed in the years of trauma, war, and abuse. Those were the true victims, at least how I grew up understanding the idea of victimhood. My family was already on the other side of the ocean when that happened. My family did not live through that. My family rebuilt, and even if they'd lost a lot, it was all just material; none of it was permanent. My family moved forward, just the way you're supposed to in America. They never looked back in any depth, never regretted the move, and were always extremely aware of the fortune they had to build the rest of their lives in the United States.

As I dug deeper into this story, as I traced my great-grandmother and great-aunt's flight, and as I discovered Hans, I found my head swimming in circles about what it all meant. I asked myself the same questions day in and day out as I found bits and pieces of more information. Finally, the blurry picture started to come into focus. I shared my discoveries with my mother since they were, of course, her family members, too, and she'd been much closer to them than I ever would be. She was still guarded but seemed more and more interested, asking more questions, happy with what little I did find. Other than that, though, I was doing this on my own and it was starting to show: I made repeated journeys down the same rabbit holes, trying to ensure I left no stone unturned. I started to feel frazzled, anxious. I started to second-guess myself, and why I was bothering with any of this at all.

Being stuck in my head is not a place I enjoy. It feels stagnant, claustrophobic, musty. I always end up at a point where I'm banging my head against the metaphorical walls, screaming without saying a word. I can do a lot by myself, and I can push myself to get things done, but I know I do my best work in groups, in a community. I flourish when I feel I am a part of something much larger than myself and the work I do, when I know the bigger vision lurking beyond my sliver of the pie. It also helps when people intrinsically understand where I am coming from without having to hear the whole story from the beginning. Usually, that is because they've experienced something similar. We do not have to tell the full story because they intuitively know it already.

So I reached out. I joined some online groups, starting this process of seeking to understand what had happened to other people's families. I put out feelers and asked if people wanted to talk. So many more did than I had anticipated; I was pleasantly surprised by the immediate candor and connection. I also mentioned my research to a few people whom I had known for years because I thought they might be in similar positions and want to talk about their own family stories. They did, too. Something else I have learned over the years is that if you give people a chance to open up in confidence and security, they usually do. We all want our stories to be heard and understood.

I have spoken with men and women aged 22 to 72 who told me the stories of dozens of their family members, people who lived through their own versions of this plight. The person who went through the experience was not always the one telling the tale, though. Most of them did not, and they especially did not want it shared with their children and grandchildren. They passed along the stories they chose to tell. The children and grandchildren did their own digging. Like me. They wanted to find out what happened even if accepting it might be ugly.

Everyone in that world who has taken the time and effort to do their own digging has a level of pride, thoughtfulness, specificity, and care about what happened to their ancestors. Each could write a book like this if they wanted to. Many families have a version of me, this one person who chooses to dig deeper, organizing what they find, and sharing it with anyone who might be willing to listen and engage.

The stories are theirs to tell, but I was looking for patterns, similarities, and differences between what I had been able to find about Irma Waldapfel and the other Waldapfels and Fischers. I wanted to understand what, if anything, was unique about my family. I felt there was something different, something making me intuit – now that I knew a little bit more about them and that they still got out – that few had similar circumstances. I had a feeling that most working-class people, most older people, were not able to get out like my great-grandmother did.

Of those I spoke with, most followed a similar path with little deviation. Just talking about who knew what and when was a knotty web. This small army of amateur researchers and historians has been able to piece together twists and turns, false starts, and dead ends. They encountered years of ancestors' adaptation and rebuilding, trying to trace the threads of those who never fully reconciled to their pasts and took details to their graves. There are litanies of conscious omissions, things in the historical record that do not align with the stories or make sense. And then they tried to shine a light on the stories in the best way possible, in a way that honors what happened. Yet often, family members – complex people in their own right, even before these experiences – could not cope with them, so they created their own reality.

For the generation that fled, there are clear cases of life frozen in amber. There were people's grandparents whose closest lifelong friends ended up being those who by happenstance escaped with them on the same boats. They could not relate to anyone else in the same way; they had their own shorthand. They had ways of doing things, cultural tics like only speaking German or Yiddish with specific people in specific instances. These friends were the only ones who could really understand what they had gone through. They understood in a way that was so earth-shattering and disruptive that they had to revert back to what they saw as a language to be forgotten but the only one that could verbalize their thoughts.

In their adopted homes, despite loving where they ended up – Argentina, Australia, Canada, the United Kingdom, the United States – they told and retold stories to each other about what happened. The same stories, with the same people, around the same table, for decades until one by one everyone passed away. The children were not allowed there; these conversations were only for those who had lived through the experience and had the regrettable badge of honor of being able to tell the tale. It was no wonder my mother and my aunt did not know any details about what had happened to their grandmother and aunt.

Further down the generational line, as they integrated into these new places and societies, many people spoke of examples of conflict and overcompensation. The overcompensation in certain cases echoed what I had read about how Jews adapted to life in Vienna between the wars, trying to become part of the fabric of a new Austrian life and culture. Some families forced this new, foreign yet permanent way of life onto children as the fastest route to showing their worthiness of staying where their new roots were planted. But it left the younger generation unable to understand the full truth of their parents' experiences. Refugees sought to ensure that their children had the most typical of upbringings in their new homes: living in the right neighborhoods, playing the right sports, going to the right schools, choosing the right high-status professional career paths, being immersed in a cultural context they would never themselves fully be part of. The parents wanted a fast-track assimilation, the fastest that was humanly possible. They did not want their children hindered by visible or audible markers of difference.

Without their children understanding the reasons for this pressure or having a sympathetic context, the full-steam-ahead integration ended up harming some relationships down the line. There was understandable pushback when the molds did not always fit. Parents did not consider who their children were or might want to be, what the next generation valued, or what kind of amalgam could ease the process. There was no hybrid of a kinder, gentler assimilation, a process that could go both ways, with cultures exchanging and building each other up. There was minimal effort to incorporate any real sense of belonging to the old culture. It seemed more important to look forward, not back, no matter where they ended up, with no real regrets that they had been able to get out and move on, even if that push forward masked a very real survivor's guilt. Maybe they could not look back. It was just too painful. Life was for the living, and they were lucky to be among the living.

From talking to people whose families had these same awful experiences, I realized that this deliberate forgetting was common. This mini generation, uncomfortably thrust together in infinite permutations of trauma that shake a sense of dignity, self, and belonging to the core, did its best to move on from a time and place that only wanted them gone.

After all, what was the point of reliving or remembering a past that had been destroyed if the goal was to successfully move on? Why bother romanticizing a place when you know, beyond a shred of doubt, that your former neighbors still living there were quite happy for you to disappear so they could take your life's work and make it theirs, needing only a few bureaucratic stamps of approval? And that in many cases, they had evolved to actively hate you – for no reason other than that they could?

Once, one of the people I was talking to, whose family had also fled Vienna, said clearly, "They knew their neighbors hated them." And with that, something clicked and my confusion about my grandfather's cutting off that part of his life dissipated. On some level, he had to completely let it go. It is the collision of the American Dream to move forward with the harsh reality of nowhere else to go – going back would be too brutal. The anger and the rage would be too personal. Even if your former neighbors were nice to your face, you knew what they thought and talked about behind your back. It was all out in the open, in all its gory detail, revealed by the destruction through a thousand papercuts of an oppressive bureaucratic regime designed to soullessly strip people of their humanity in the name of a racist and fascist ideology. Which my family's neighbors happily supported. My grandfather's rejection of all things actively Austrian beyond those who gave him familiar comfort now made sense.

But eventually, we must always come to terms psychically with what has been subsumed under the mask of survival. Every culture has its unspoken guidelines, every religion its process for coming to terms with wrong and, if not making it right, at least finding peace and moving on. Every person has their own lines in the sand for what they will learn to tolerate and what they will not subject themselves to – for their own dignity and humanity. My family, it seems, was no different in that regard. And neither was anybody else's. They, too, buried the things they thought would be too difficult for their children, but their descendants found ways to unearth them anyway all those long years later.

Those were the similarities that wove through the tapestry of intimate, individual stories within the collective experience of Jews who fled Austria and Germany just in the nick of time. They were easy to see and impossible to ignore, obvious beginnings to connecting the dots. But as I spoke to more people, learned more about their particular family circumstances, and thought about how they were different from mine, the patterns began to diverge. The biggest differences emerging from these conversations were about economic class – the haves and have-nots. Most of whom I spoke with were the descendants of the haves – and that reality is indelibly linked to whose stories are ultimately told and see the light of day.

For most I spoke with whose families were able to escape in that first wave preceding Kristallnacht – the eight months after the Anschluss when the Nazi apparatus was being formalized in Austria – the stories were about people from wealthier backgrounds. These ancestors were factory owners, large business owners, and international distributors. They were doctors, lawyers, and teachers. They were respectable, locally known members of society. Family lore passed down had them reacting to events differently, but at least at the beginning, they never questioned whether they could leave. They struggled with whether they wanted to leave and whether it made sense considering their vested interests in Vienna, the lives they built, and the local connections they thought they needed to maintain. They were questions more about maintaining bourgeois assets and lifestyles, not about survival, mistrust of the authorities, or if life as they knew it would devolve into catastrophe.

For some of these wealthier families, it meant that the older generations stayed because the idea of leaving it all behind and beginning again felt too difficult. Only the younger generation of the time left – those without that sense of permanence but with some family money as a cushion or guarantee. They were a mere handful of young men and women from their comfortably small tribes who left unaware they would never see their parents and grandparents again. Once the danger became acute in a very existential way where life and limb were physically threatened, it was too late to leave. What might have worked in the beginning, in terms of relinquishing property and paying exorbitant fees for the privilege of running for their lives, was no longer an option. The vise was already too tight and was about to get tighter.

However, for others who tried to leave from the beginning, it meant that large families were able to get out together. Some of these wealthier families were able to exit Nazi Austria, get travel permits to whatever country would take them, and end up in random parts of the world together. In transit, they subsisted on what residual savings and day labor they could patch together for undetermined lengths of time, which ended up being years. But they remained as family units amid all the chaos and uncertainty. Those stories amaze me – people who traveled anywhere in the world where they felt they would be safe, holding on for years when the only certainty was unpredictability and the likeliness of having to move again. Many wound up in seemingly exotic places such as India, Shanghai, or Caracas until the next passage became available.

There was another category: those whose level of wealth and establishment into society meant assimilation. They did not even know they were considered Jewish until the Nazis informed them. They took commonly held beliefs like antisemitism as universal truths because they were not Jewish in any practical sense and did not comprehend what it meant to belong to this ethnic group or practice its religion. Maybe they had one or two Jewish grandparents, but that was a long time ago, and they viewed themselves as regular, wealthy Austrians, part of the normal, staid cotton and wool of society. They could not be considered self-hating Jews because neither they nor the established Jewish community considered them Jewish. They were Austrian Catholics just like everyone else in their milieu. And then, suddenly, their reality completely changed because of a bureaucratic designation they never thought applied to them. Then it was too late.

Some descendants of wealthy families mentioned in passing that a partner or spouse of someone who got out was not wealthy, but, ultimately, their exodus was also made possible by family wealth. My family clearly was not wealthy, an apparently rare circumstance in terms of who was able to legally flee Austria in 1938. I kept asking myself, "Why were they ultimately successful when so many other working-class people, especially if they were also older, were not?"

If I think about my family's background, if I go back a bit before that code red emergency in 1938, I think that a large part of my family's approach to things was likely because of where my great-grandparents came from within the empire, and how my grandfather and his siblings grew up. They were working-class, assimilated Jews who were able to realistically assess the coming danger with enough time to make a plan and secure the resources to leave despite limitations they had. They were able to put it into action despite being separated by an ocean, with restricted information going in and coming out, having not seen each other for a decade. They were able to make things move to bring the people who were in a dire situation to a better place. None of this was guaranteed to be successful, and none of it could be taken for granted.

My great-grandparents came from a subregion in Central Europe at the nexus of what are now the Czech, Slovak, and Polish borders – three modern-day countries – and double the number of languages were spoken there at the time. Maybe there was something about that place and how it might have informed their sense of being able to belong anywhere if it felt right and allowed them to survive. Maybe there was a lack of stability there when they were coming of age that made them seek out options and opportunities and forced them to be flexible. Maybe there was an attitude toward life that allowed them to trust their instincts about when it was time to pull up stakes and move on to wherever they could survive.

After spending the early part of their married life working and trading in progressively larger Slovak and Czech market towns, my great-grandparents made the move to Vienna with three small children. In Vienna, my family clearly had migrated recently from within the Austro-Hungarian Empire, living in Hernals, the city's far-flung 17th District, which snakes northwest, out and up to the boundary of the Viennese Woods that marks its tail end. It was a relatively new addition to the city proper and had been retrofitted and built out for these types of arrivals only 15 years or so before their arrival. Hernals, which has its own Viennese way of living and still incorporates such newly arrived working-class denizens, was far removed physically and in attitude from Leopoldstadt, the 2nd District, on the opposite side of the city.

Leopoldstadt, I would argue, has the same place in the historical imagination of urban Jewish migration to Vienna as the Lower East Side of Manhattan in New York City does as its country's epicenter of a Jewish-centric cultural fusion. But the Lower East Side has housed waves and waves of recently arrived immigrants to New York, not just Jews, all of whom tended to move to parts of the city with more amenable housing options as soon as they could. Many Jews in Leopoldstadt, on the other hand, stayed even as they achieved wealth and societal integration because it built up respectability as a cultural center. My family did not live in Leopoldstadt, and as far as I know, did not experience much of its cultural rush. They had some scattered family in the city to support and cushion their landing, but their family ties to what later became Czechoslovakia and then broke apart again seem to have been stronger than to Vienna. They do not seem to have had a strong connection to the way of life preserved in the history books as the "typical" story of Viennese Jews.

My great-grandparents were working-class Jews, to be sure, but ones actively seeking opportunity. They had enough resources and support to have moved to Vienna out of expediency, with three small children for whom they wanted more. They wanted their children to have better opportunities than they would have in Slovakia or Moravia. They were already in flux, in a sense, without the ties that bound them to Vienna, yet they looked for stability, a place where their hard work would be rewarded and they could be respected. When they moved, Vienna was the only place in the Empire that could have enticed them with that promise. Even though Vienna treated them well enough, considering their humble origins, they were not bound to it like the wealthy were. And they knew they could move on and change if they had to because they had done it before.

My family's lives do not seem to have been particularly defined by their Jewish identity. My grandfather and his siblings grew up as regular Viennese children in ethnically mixed, working-class Hernals. But back then, there was no neutral secular state that we take for granted today in Western democracies. Their civil documents were still issued by the Israelitische Kultusgemeinde [Jewish

Religious Community], official arbiters of all things Jewish in Vienna to this day.

My family integrated as well as possible in Vienna given the opportunities available. The next generation, my grandfather and his siblings, who could grow up there like natives without a foreign accent, went to high school and trade school, not university. Then, they tried to start working. However, structural barriers limited their opportunities. When the time came to determine where their future would be, if not exactly what it would look like, my great-uncle, great-aunt, and grandfather each took a look around with clear eyes. Without exception, they chose to leave Europe, not expecting to return.

Perhaps all of these factors explain why they did not view integrating into the United States as an insurmountable barrier. They were already used to blending in with a larger culture that was different but not totally foreign. And they were already used to getting by in difficult or unexpected circumstances because they had to. Something in them allowed them to move through the world while retaining the essence of who they were.

I want to think that perhaps, with so much of life mobile and in flux, their sense of home was a mutable place. Maybe home was wherever they were, together, whether it was Slovakia, Moravia, Czechia, Austria, or the United States. Maybe for them, home was defined less by place. Not because they wanted to wander but because life had taught them to recognize when a given place could not allow them to grow, in the stubborn, relentlessly human ways they wanted to, in the ways that an underclass is always banging up against in our modern societies.

Their mobility within, and then out of, the Austro-Hungarian Empire sets the backdrop. It helps me try to understand where they came from, and why they were different from most other Viennese Jews – even those who got out, whose descendants I now know and tell their own stories. Truth be told, I fit in with those other descendants as well because, unlike my working-class Viennese ancestors, my parents were part of the middle and upper-middle class before I was born. I have a master's degree and a professional career. However, if with my current level of education and career trajectory I had been in my family's circumstances in 1938 Vienna, I would have found it difficult to leave my established networks to face the unknown. I would have landed on the side of the bourgeoisie, and I probably would have held off on leaving until it was nearly too late, if I had been able to get out at all.

The importance of this difference in class that I see with my family is simple. If the searching that had been part of my family's way of seeing the world for decades hadn't somehow informed a level of urgency from the branch of the family already on the other side of the Atlantic, there is no way my great-grandmother and great-aunt would have been able to get everything in order so quickly and leave within weeks. If their departure, both pushed and facilitated by their American brethren, hadn't been in the works by March 1938, I am completely, totally, utterly convinced they would not have been able to get out. They were only able to flee because they had family already living in the United States terrified of what would happen to them. The upper middle classes did not, for the most part, have this preexisting network of family abroad to deeply care, sound the alarm bells as the vise appeared to tighten, and then pave the way for their departure.

As things fell apart for Jews in Austria in 1938, as tangible property and connections became currency, as lines formed to be able to get out, and bribery became the easiest way to achieve it, my family would not have been able to access this new way of making things happen. They lacked the financial resources. Sigmund Freud, perhaps Jewish Vienna's best-known representative of the time, got everything together for his family's departure, signed away most of his assets, and fled a week before my family did, on June 4, 1938. My family certainly was not of that milieu. Although they migrated to Vienna from the same part of Moravia and lived a 40-minute walk away from him in Vienna, I would wager a princely sum of money it was no coincidence that they never crossed paths.

Without the preparation and push from the younger generation in New York, there is no way that Irma and Karoline Waldapfel would have been out on June 12, 1938. Not with the very few cards they had to play. Even if, on the other side of the world, nobody wanted to talk about it later.

Even if my family members were outliers in that they got out when they did, especially considering their class, they were not outliers in moving on and looking back as little as possible. That seems to be what most people did, albeit with the cultural elements that stuck, like accents, food choices, or artistic preferences, the smaller and larger signs that they came from another world that they kept firmly in the rear-view mirror.

The last official documentation that I was able to get from that era, to piece together what had happened, drove a definitive and final nail into my research. It came, surprisingly, directly from the Austrians. I learned about it late in my process of fitting the puzzle pieces together. There is a database search mechanism that scrapes different archives that the Austrian state has for anything related to the Nazi regime and its victims called the Findbuch. Once I found out about it, I requested an account and typed Irma Waldapfel into a search bar for what felt like the millionth time. I was tired of searching for her and hoping that something newly relevant would magically appear. Our petition had already been submitted, so I was not going to add any other documentation to our file. I searched for her again simply to ensure that no stone was left unturned.

And somehow, almost magically this time, there she was, again. She would exist, in perpetuity, in a special set of Austrian State Archives holdings specifically for compensations and restitutions related to state seizure of property after the nation comfortably folded itself into the Nazi Reich. Or, more formally, from the Aryanization files of the Property Transaction Office of Vienna.

These files were not digitized, but I wrote to the general email address that the Findbuch search engine included for those archives. I requested a full copy of whatever might be there, for myself, for my family, for our understanding of what might have happened. Again, I did not have high expectations for what would happen. I was pleasantly surprised when, a few months later, a polite email came back asking to verify the mailing address where these files could be sent. And then, a few weeks after that, a much thicker envelope than I would have expected arrived in our mailbox with that nation's now-familiar red-and-white flag on the return address.

I opened it at the dining room table where so much of this work had already happened and began to sift through it, using the Google Translate app to complement my limited German. There appeared to be two very different sets of documents. The first, which the dates indicate must have been executed in absentia because my great-grandmother had already fled, was about the transfer of that small liquor store and bar, all that was left of their material property in Vienna, to Johann Thaler and his wife, who appeared to be neighbors. The 25 pages of documentation validated that he was someone who was rising in the ranks, a trustworthy Nazi deemed to be of high enough moral character and worthiness to merit taking over the shop and its physical goods. They also included that he had limited funds and needed formal approval of the sale from the Nazi authorities as soon as possible to retain solvency. Poor guy.

The second set of documents was from much later, after 1955, when the reconstituted Austrian Republic set up the first of a series of restitution options. There was a formal petition for restitution, notarized in New York, submitted for the full value of that same property. There was a letter written by my great-aunt Valerie on behalf of her mother summarizing the situation and requesting that her mother, now in her 80s, be compensated fairly by the authorities. And there were records of two wire transfers, from the then-new Austrian government, totaling about $12,000 in today's dollars in response. I do not know if that was as fair as they would have liked, or what the fair market value of that type of business in that neighborhood would be now, but it was better than nothing, certainly better than the measly $4,000 they got in 1938, which paid for their passage to the United States and left virtually nothing else for when they arrived.

I thought a lot about trying to find Johann Thaler, but that is an extremely common name in the German-speaking world. It would be very difficult now to find that particular Johann Thaler, from that particular place, especially if he was an otherwise undistinguished neighbor and then blended back into Viennese or Austrian society after the war. I thought a lot about the full compensation that my great-grandmother received, for a business that had sustained her family for a full generation and was ultimately assigned a full value in today's money of about $16,000. To me, that felt marginal, like a slap in the face for 30 years of work and a terrifyingly uncertain process of self-removal, which they were lucky to even be able to do.

That was how it formally ended for them 20 years after they fled. The restitution fund cut a couple of small checks and called it a day. After that, there doesn't seem to have been much more to say about the matter, which was closed out. They were recognized, they were compensated. It was not much, but they took the money and walked away. The man who – lucky for him – harvested what they had sowed, likely stayed put, and got along just fine both during and after the war.

I thought about digging deeper, but I could not. I asked myself, Why should I bother? Why should I dig deeper, chasing down these last little tendrils of the story? What good would it do me or anyone else? I know what happened. I know they were just small fish in this huge pond of injustice, that they got out, and that years later, it was formally and financially recognized that something bad happened to them. And that must be enough for now. The specific systems that allowed it to happen had closed the books.

What good, what sort of productive, progressive end, could come out of me chasing down old and elusive ghosts, even if I could find them, and pointing fingers at people who are so far removed from what their great-grandparents did that they would just be confused about it? Especially since everyone did it at the time. None.

No good, none at all, in the same way that trying to comprehensively track down what happened to dozens of Waldapfels and Fischers in Czechoslovakia after 1939 was a fool's errand, leading down a black hole of anger and grief about something that happened nearly a century ago. There was no point in going further down this pathway for me, and there hadn't been for them, either. It was over. Broken into a million pieces, never to be fully put back together. *Kaput*.

In my family's case, forgetting this story, letting it go, allowed everyone to move on and become American without any love lost for the world they had left behind and knew was gone, with the people and places they had loved destroyed. It allowed the younger generations – my mother and aunt, myself and my cousins – to move, integrated and accent-free, within the structure of American society. Untethered to ghosts that other immigrant groups escaping from atrocity – including those who actually experienced the war, the camps, and arrived ten years further down the line – never completely escaped. It allowed them to cut the cord and build life anew in a country that venerates the ideal that people begin fresh once they land on American soil. In places and times that very much welcome forgetting uncomfortable truths once the stories are no longer told.

These types of stories now get forgotten more quickly than they did before, although frequently enough there are at least archives around for anyone who wants to look. And there is certainly enough information to go on, even if not all the pieces of the puzzle can ever be clicked into place. But now I am sure that, for some people, it is so much easier to never know. Maybe they're too close to the horror of what happened and find that ignorance is easier to manage. Maybe they never quite forget but find a new reality that keeps the raw wound at bay, which eventually scabs and scars over. There may always be a reminder, but it is baked into who they are, who they're becoming, and it is easier to ignore since it is just an ugly mark that fades with time. They probably talk about it with the people who were there at the time, but why burden those who are innocent and did not live through those awful realities? Hopefully, those innocents will never experience anything so dire.

For me, all these years down the line, even if I'll never know exactly what happened, my ability to fill in important gaps in the story created an important understanding of the process of my applying for Austrian citizenship and why it is important. Why, in fact, my family members were victims, even if they would not have given themselves that label, or actively identified themselves as such. It gives me a way to bring dimension, color, and life to the vague stories I had heard over the years and think about what I would have done in their shoes, how I would have coped. What kind of anxiety and desperation they likely felt, not knowing if things would work out. How difficult the resettlement process was, trying to assimilate but knowing that, at a certain point, it is hard to start over when you are older. Writing this, I am about the age my great-aunt Valerie was when she had to coordinate her mother and sister's flight from afar and accommodate them in their new homeland as they became American themselves. How would I handle that level of trust, that level of responsibility? I am sure I would be able to, just as she did, but the truth is you do not know until you're forced. And nobody wants to be forced.

It gives me another sense of these pictures and legends as people, just like me and my friends, doing the best they could, which ended up being more than fine. I hope they would be happy with me wondering about them, finding out as much as I could about their lives, much of which I am sure they would rather have forgotten. I do not think anyone wants to be remembered for posterity only in the context of the most difficult part of their lives. But knowing that they lived through this experience, and were able to flourish afterward, they give me the strength to navigate anything that may happen. I know that, if they were able to find a way out, a way forward, I will be able, too, no matter what.

PART III
PRESENT

XI. THE PATH FORWARD

In the beginning, it was just about the citizenship, and the ways that that would have changed my own life and trajectory, had I had it when I was younger. When I saw the news and thought about how it might apply to me, my reaction was linear. Get me from point A to point B. Give me an open door and justification to freely live in different ways and different places that I felt had eluded me for so long. I, too, could find myself among the people whose options I had coveted – to move from here to there just because they felt like it. At that point, I had already made an international life for myself as an American, and I did not need a burgundy passport. But the possibility still gnawed at me.

As a child, for many years I had never really considered there were things to question about myself or my place in the world, or about where I belonged or felt like I could belong. Growing up in the calm and peaceful American suburbs where things felt immutable and permanent was a privilege. I know that now. But then it was just the way things were. It was completely normal for my grandparents to live in the same place for decades with my long-deceased great-grandmother still listed on the apartment's nameplate. It was normal to get in the car and trust there would always be money to keep up with the annual verification checks, get it registered, and have a full tank of gas. It was normal to think that we could always go to a retail store and get new clothes, new toys, and only have to think of cost in a superficial way. Even though in practice we balked at paying full price at expensive shops because, culturally, we would not spend extra money on things we did not have to; that way, we could spend it on things we did want to.

I was traveling from an early age, whether it was a couple hours from our spacious ranch house to my grandparents' apartment in South Brooklyn or the oceanside for a day or two, or a longer trip to Montreal to visit my cousins where they spoke a different language and used different colored money and measured distances differently as soon as you crossed a real but arbitrary line. That was all very normal, even if the car rides were long or we always went to the same places to visit family. And my parents, my father in particular, pushed me to experience life beyond the eight hours of interstate with forking pathways between Washington and Boston, so I did not think that way of life was the only way mine could go. The travel, the curiosity, the knowing other worlds, and other ways were all baked into how I grew up.

At 15, which I know now is quite young even though I felt more than old enough at the time, I began to travel internationally on my own. First, I traveled for academics. I was part of a cluster of about a dozen overexcited teenagers, converging from different parts of the US, on the same red-eye Aer Lingus flight out of Boston to go to a summer program at a Dublin university campus. Whether my parents intended it to happen or not, Ireland was just different enough, the people I met just exciting enough, and just open enough to me, to really turbocharge my already-ignited travel bug.

Since the language was the same, I could navigate the personal elements of the trip and place just fine. I adopted a different cadence in my voice when speaking to people with Irish accents that felt magical, like it came out of nowhere. The most exotic parts of otherwise mundane daily life that enthralled me were the meandering Dublin roads with architectural styles I had never seen before, and groceries that were different from what we had back home, especially the junk food. In retrospect, the social hierarchies were likely as constricted as where I came from, if not moreso. But since I had no context for the Irish, and they had no context for me, it all felt like a blank slate. I later learned that some of my friends from this era came from politically elite and wildly rich families – a level of wealth and power that far surpassed anyone I had ever met in my suburban American existence. But money or proximity to power meant nothing to me. For me, these people were intriguing, fun, and smart. They seemed far more interesting and worldly than those I knew at home. To top it off, they were nice to me. And that was all I needed.

That was probably the point when I started to think that others' lives were more interesting than my own. That to go somewhere else, to learn something else, to experience someone else brought a heightened sense of reality at the same time it brought a feeling of personal smallness. I had the feeling that the world was so vast, so endless, that I could never experience it all. But I could try to experience more of it, as much of it as I could. I could try to eat it all up and see how much I could chew. My normal life, the way I grew up, seemed boring and secondary to all these other things outside myself. This did not negate, or even change, my identity. I have always known who I am, always known where I am from. But everything else seemed so much more colorful, so much more fun to explore.

It is only now that I am starting to realize and open up to the idea that my life is, and has always been, just as intriguing and engaging as these other people's lives. For many years, I would not let myself believe that. The other was always better, more interesting, more worthy. I felt uncomfortable analyzing myself because I could always find flaws and feel like I could do more or do things better. It is easier to listen to others and think about them, in their own world and words, and reflect the best version of that back onto them. It has been a long journey to love myself enough to reflect that same worth back onto myself. I still do not know if I am completely there, but I try. And I try to be present in my life, without looking too far forward or backward, and be appreciative and accepting of all of the complexity that makes me *me*.

I am sure that my international experiences helped me immediately feel at home in proudly multicultural, multilingual, and international Montreal. While in university, I wanted to be able to move through an exciting city with endless neighborhoods to explore, delicious yet affordable food, and too many cultural activities to count. Montreal fit the bill perfectly. I gained acceptance to McGill University and did not look back even though my guidance counselor at school fretted that I could have gone to an Ivy League school and did not even bother to apply. Her attitude was more reflective of the wealthier suburbs in the Boston-to-Washington stretch of Interstate 95 where maintaining a relatively elite status was the focal point of "good" high schools like the one I excelled in, which trained students to take their places as the backbone of the white-collar status quo. My own limited experience, even up until that point, had shown me there was more out there than what my high school guidance counselor wanted me to plug into.

By the time I was settled in and comfortable with my university experience in bustling downtown Montreal, with comprehensive access throughout the city by metro and bus, I could easily navigate the complexities of meeting people from all over the world. Montreal was still relatively affordable for most in the early 2000s; this was when video-game and other technology companies were buying old warehouses to convert to offices and coming in. Post-manufacturing Montreal was, at that stage, still a little grimy. It was still figuring out the type of city it would become. There were longstanding festivals that brought in tourists, but the newer structure of this port city on an island, as New York was, was still in flux. As was I.

I taught myself to move in and out of social circles, work environments, cafés, and music festivals with people whom I could have only met in that place at that time, who wanted to live peaceful lives while enjoying them to the fullest. For many people, it was easy enough to immigrate to Canada at the time, so they did. They brought their own food with them, which could be found in an endless supply of international restaurants that I happily explored. They brought their own traditions, which were harder to come across unless you got to know people on a more personal, nonjudgmental level. An approach centered on kind curiosity that showed you were simply interested in them as a person. Then, over time, they opened up and might tell you a bit about where they came from, or ask you to meet them at one of their favorite cafés in another part of the city that reminded them, and many others like them, of the home they were not sure they would see again. I listened to these stories with rapt attention, startled, for example, to hear friends from the Middle East commiserate with each other that they could never enjoy firework displays after growing up hearing bombs drop during regional wars. These events that were a footnote in my awareness of the world were still real for them.

I also had friends with multiple nationalities who were clear about them and saw these nationalities as complementary and additive, not something to hide behind. One friend was Italian Canadian American, another was Hungarian Canadian, and yet another Polish Canadian. I am sure there were others as well. Those multiple nationalities, I learned at the time, were all through family descendance pathways. After the experiences I had seeing that those other worlds and places could be wonderfully exciting, first in Ireland and then Canada – where I wanted to stay a little longer but wasn't sure I could – I was envious that my friends could make those choices for themselves. I was not resentful in the slightest. I was happy for them, their options, their choices. But I wanted those choices for myself, and they were not mine. I wanted to have that power for myself. To just pick up and go because I could. To have the kind of personal growth that is, fundamentally, central to the American Dream.

I did not know what or where I wanted to be, but I wanted to carve out my own path even if it felt more cumbersome and difficult – and sometimes unnecessary. To the surprise of everyone, including myself, I ended up in Mexico for a long time. I continue to keep it as a home. With a little bit of inheritance money and the hubris that comes from being 22, unstoppable, and clueless, armed with a powerful passport and a recommendation for a nice town to live in from my father (who had been there on business multiple times), I found a language school online that offered three-month immersion courses and bought a one-way ticket. What I thought would be three months ended up stretching for two and a half years, and then beyond that, over time.

I have ended up working throughout the American continent, having friends and colleagues from Chile to Canada and most places in between. I have traveled both for work and pleasure. Peru and Panama and Puerto Rico; La Paz and Limón. As I have opened myself up, the Americas have become accessible and open to me in a way I never would have expected, never would have attempted, and never would have felt comfortable with had I just stayed where I grew up. If I can navigate so many different spaces in all their complexity and come out relatively unscathed – well, I can navigate anything.

My American experiences have been less of a travelog and more of a sense of discovery mixed with surprise and awe. Who am I to be welcomed to these places? What did I do to wake up one morning at a colleague's cousin's house on a cove facing out to the Atlantic, with an errant sloth lazing six feet away in a tree? Nothing, really. I have done nothing to deserve this welcome, other than come in with openness and curiosity and thoughts that I can now express with moderation and thoughtfulness, not just trying to get along. These episodes of both expected and unexpected intimacy are out of goodwill and hospitality, not an unspoken quid pro quo. Friends and colleagues know I will happily return the favor should they find themselves in places where I have similar amenities that I can offer to them. There is no short-term trade-off and no expectation that there will be. The world is bigger, more welcoming.

These genuine connections and friendships do not happen with everyone. Nor do they happen all the time. But when they do, when you can cultivate care and understanding, they allow for golden moments where you look out over the sea, the mountains, or the plains, wherever you are in that place and time, and say to yourself, "I am just so lucky in this world." And you keep those moments as a sacred treasure for yourself, content in both the beauty and the transience of the moments, places, and friendships. When you haven't had them before, they are wonderful moments to remember.

In a way, I have a special kind of peace and privilege to feel American in the broadest sense of the word. Understanding both the promise and frustration of that American Dream of individual peace and prosperity. How it can manifest in so many ways, in so many different countries, whose initial similarity was only just being on this side of the world. The Americas are – writ large – bound to that promise. In unbinding the once-dominant millenary cultures that have barely survived European colonization, countries of all political persuasions have opened up the chaotic floodgates of individualism in ways that did not evolve in most other parts of the world.

In the Americas, many seem to think that the promise of individual reward is so great that it shunts aside the learnings of different types of societies that are calmer, cooler, and more collective. In these societies, there will also always be winners and losers, heroes and villains, but the price isn't necessarily so high, and the winner doesn't have to take everything. Each country has done this differently, with its own particularly peculiar history informing the way modern countries engage with themselves, each other and the broader world. But the promise of bounty in the Americas is still there, the promise and possibility that keeps people coming.

My American privilege can take on many forms. It is the peace of freely living, traveling through borders both mental and mapped out, without questioning whether I will get through or how I will manage it. It is the comfort of regularly passing through barriers physical and imagined without a second glance. It is the ability to command at least some respect – more than most women in most parts of the world – when I open my mouth and words flow out.

I wonder what my immigrant ancestors, first called economic migrants and then refugees, coming from places that were volatile and complex, would think, seeing how easy all this is for me, knowing how difficult it was for them. If this is what they had wanted for themselves, or if they had just wanted something quieter, more peaceful, without the added complexity that I seem to seek out for myself. If they had just wanted that little corner of the world where they would not be threatened just for being born who they were. Or I wonder if they would recognize unrealized parts of themselves in me. I wonder if they would have liked to go along for this ride. I wonder if they would have liked the person I am today.

XII. PROVING THE LINK

One aspect is the personal, the feelings of what we want, what's fair, what people experience, the way we internalize everything within our consciousness and subconsciousness. The other is the political, the administrative, the bureaucratic, what we are allowed to do, and the processes we must follow. One lives in our heads and our hearts. The other lives on paper and is stamped along a procedural assembly line by people following rules and policies that we rarely know unless, for some strange reason, we've also held those exact jobs, and the policies haven't changed very much since.

The application pathway Austria was laying out for this new citizenship-by-descent option, which I first tried to understand in the fall of 2020, did not initially seem difficult for someone like me, having managed my own visa applications and approvals in other contexts. In fact, I had managed them many times throughout my adult life: first in Canada, then in Ireland when I was back for a few months just after finishing university, and then several times in Mexico. These kinds of processes might prove long and tedious, but they are not hard or impossible if you do your research beforehand. If you know you have some formal documents that substantively support what these places seem to be requesting. If, before you set out to chart the course, you can fill out the forms you need to submit, pay the necessary fees, and trust you will ultimately get back the certified documents to submit to the authorities where you are going. Within these documents, in the best-case scenario, there might also be responses you are seeking to questions you do not know how to answer.

Knowing the logistics and machinations of one's family's path as I did, or at least where to start looking, made me feel the pathway laid out by Austria seemed feasible. The process also needed some extra certifications and apostilles, a form of authentication for documents to be recognized internationally. I started mapping out where I could begin to request documents online. Upon learning where I would then need to send the documents to get the extra levels of certification, it seemed like a tediously precise but straightforward process.

The Austrians would start every case with what they were calling a "persecuted ancestor." This person was the root of the case, and if you were not clear on your persecuted ancestor, you would not get very far. They had to be all of the following: Austrian or a citizen of one of the other countries that splintered out from the Austro-Hungarian Empire; a documented resident of Austria before fleeing the country; and a victim of persecution from the fascist regimes of the time. So who was this person, and could you prove they were persecuted? About whom in your direct family lineage could you say, "They suffered because of how the state treated them, now make this right." All this even though my family members never would have considered themselves victims. Persecuted, maybe. Victims, definitively no.

The Austrians included a laundry list of potential documents that would be helpful to include about this persecuted ancestor but did not clearly say how many of them, or which specific documents, were needed:

- Birth certificate

- Proof of citizenship: passport or certificate of citizenship
- Proof of residence: registration [*Meldezettel*], confirmation by a refugee camp, and so on
- Documents that indicate the date of the departure from Austria, including supporting documentation/evidence that your persecuted ancestor received abroad, like an entry form, a residence registration form, proof of military service, university enrollment certificate, and so on.
- Proof of persecution (victim card) [*Opferausweis*], Austrian pension payments, documents from the National Fund of the Republic of Austria for Victims of National Socialism or the General Settlement Fund for Victims of National Socialism)
- Decisions of Austrian authorities if your ancestor regained his citizenship

Well, we had ... some of that? Probably? We had the passport, which written inside had my great-grandmother's last Austrian address – her official residence for 30 years. We did not have her birth certificate, but I imagined the passport could not have been issued without a birth certificate from somewhere, even if that country hadn't existed for a hundred years. The passport also had her date of departure, with her visas meticulously stamped before there were the computerized systems of today to automatically validate that level of detail. Maybe I could find information on the American side about when she arrived and was naturalized.

On the Austrian side, my mother hazily recalled that many years before, she thought that her grandmother had gotten some recompense (which, we later found out, was the restitution for the forced sale of her liquor store and bar). However, we did not initially have anything on paper to substantiate the family legends and stories from a world away. Maybe, though, the Austrians did. We did not know what was in their public and private archives, or what additional registers and databases they might have access to that we could not. It might be a little tricky, and a little more complicated, but it did not seem impossible. Maybe we did have a reasonable shot at becoming Austrian.

Then, after establishing my great-grandmother's identity as an Austrian, the challenge would be to prove our official family lineage using those finicky, bureaucratic, civil registry documents that list your parents on them, to trace upstream or downstream as needed. I learned quickly there are only three types of public documents likely to have this type of information clearly marked, registered by all relevant authorities for all time. Those documents that mark life's greatest hits: birth, marriage, and death certificates.

After hopefully substantiating my great-grandmother in a way the Austrians would accept as one of them, what were the documents we'd need for other family members? For my grandfather – her son – we did not have a birth certificate, and I was not sure we could get it. He was born in what was then called Oderfurt, within the Austro-Hungarian Empire, and now called Přívoz. It is a nearby suburb of Ostrava, the third-largest city in modern-day Czechia. From what I could tell on the map, Přívoz looked to be Cambridge to Ostrava's Boston. But between the three changes of country and two changes of city name since my grandfather's 1907 birth, it seemed like it would be very complicated to get his original birth certificate. Plus, there was the problem of logistics. I did not know anyone who spoke Czech or could help us figure out what documentation had been destroyed during both World War I and World War II, and what, if anything, would potentially be in the public domain, a public record I would not need a specific justification to ask for. If it was not in the public domain, we would probably have to figure out how to get into 100-plus-year-old archives, and there would be no telling how long trying to find his birth certificate could take. If we could even successfully find it. I hoped we would not need it.

I thought about other documents we could use to prove ancestry and that family connection. I wondered if something slightly less formal still existed in Vienna such as school records, with parental consent for enrollment or authorization that he could be involved in some sort of activity. I had some of those old forms for myself, from my own school records, and knew there were variations in how long they had to be stored by different authorities. But without knowing how the Austrians kept such records, if they even did, or the names of the schools he attended in Vienna, that seemed overwhelming, too.

Running through the different options for sourcing old European documents, it seemed like a lost cause to try to source them for both my great-grandmother and my grandfather, and I hoped it would not be necessary. I would have to rely on what they had done once they arrived in the United States. If birth certificates were not an option, it would have to be marriage licenses, death certificates, or both if we could. Did the Austrians need both for my grandfather? Or would that just be overkill? I hoped we could get them easily, although I was not sure how to access them. I also hoped that getting my mother's birth certificate and marriage license, and a new long-form copy of my birth certificate, would not be too hard.

As it turned out, Austria's waiting 80 years to offer restitution citizenship made pulling some parts of the slurry of documentation together easier than it would have otherwise been. Genealogy has grown so much easier over the years, something I realized as I learned so much about different kinds of public records at all levels of government. I learned how much is available online. Sometimes you have to shop around on the different genealogy websites – Ancestry, Geni, FamilySearch, or other, more niche, search engines – to find what you're looking for, but most of it is there somewhere. Even without anyone in my immediate family being into genealogy themselves, there are extensive family trees that my people are somehow branched out into, latched on in the periphery. So many people have put so much time and effort into tracking people they never knew, people to whom they were only tangentially connected, in a sort of metaphysical scavenger hunt across time and place.

I learned that for the most part, after 75 years in the US and 110 years in Austria, many local vital records for my family were accessible and federal records available. And all of these genealogy sites have some way to scoop them up, scan them, and make them all accessible from the comfort of your own desk, behind your own computer screen, or your own cellphone or tablet, if you happen to want to access this information while you're on the move. I learned that – despite war, bombing, and destruction – many records remain, to the extent that it is possible to put the pieces together. All you need is a starting point with some very concrete information – like we had with the passports – and know more or less how to use a search function. So much time, money, and effort have been put into making this information accessible. At least with these types of archives.

So as I got started, it turned out easier to find many things than I had ever imagined. And the easiest of them all, strangely enough, were my great-grandmother, grandfather, and great-aunt's petitions for naturalization in the United States. They were short files – three or four pages – scanned from federal archives. They had basic biodata filled into a standard format and snapshots that echoed mugshots, but without the numbers and the anger, just a neutral, somewhat tired, resignation on their faces.

For them, these documents hopefully would be the last step in processes that were long, arduous, psychologically taxing, and always uncertain until the papers were approved. This was another set of photographs that showed they were who they always claimed to be, another set of documentation that provided the same information about where they had come from and to whom they were related. These were the documents to give the strangers that populated the bureaucratic machine from which they hoped to come out on the right side, proving the skeleton outline of their lives. I saw in their faces, looking straight forward and devoid of real emotion, expressions that reflected the exhaustion within that unknown, hoping this would be the last time they had to fill out similar forms, with the same information, and submit them to the discretion of the black box of an unknown bureaucracy just to allow them to live their lives. Hopefully, this set of paperwork would finally be enough.

It was jarring to see my grandfather, in his portly mid-30s, staring directly out at me like that. I would not have recognized him on the street, not looking like that, not even if he came up and started talking to me about things that only he would know, only we could know together. But there he was. And there was his sister, and there was his mother, all neatly adjudicated and approved, deemed to become United States citizens by the Southern District of New York. The documents were just a few immediate clicks away for me even though the process had taken years for them.

I quickly found other records, too, without needing to look very hard. From different databases that had been consolidated within these genealogical websites, I found different ship manifests. I found entry records. I found draft cards. I found census records. I found marriage licenses. I found birth registries written in elaborate script in German and English. I found old Social Security numbers. I found death records. I found all of these records from different jurisdictions across states, countries, and continents. I could not believe it was now so easy to piece together the complex personal details of people who had, in my experience, been so private.

I found the bureaucratic pieces of life that showed movement, that showed change, that showed the procession of ordinary lives in both ordinary and extraordinary times. People have always been born, lived their lives, and died, but there was not always the apparatus at a global level to preserve these big moments when people are forced to interact with public institutions – institutions that may have changed and in some cases became the apparatus of war and destruction. I thought about being in my own science-fiction movie and time-traveling to show some of the documents to these people as I was rediscovering these moments in their lives. As they were living through these changes, they would remember the details, and they would be able to color in the vague sketches I was able to draw. I wondered what they would think about the records being saved for an undetermined posterity, eventually available for anyone in the world to explore.

I also figured out how to request all these different documents that were not yet in the public domain, that might be useful in very different ways from the practical to the psychic, from their archival places of origin. As long as I was in the middle of this journey, it seemed like good practice to access everything we could and have physical, printed copies on hand. As I was experiencing, you never know what you might need in the future, what you would want to have available in the long term, and what documents there might be a need for that nobody would have anticipated.

Snap out of it. Organize yourself. There is a point to all this, a goal. Come down from that cloud up at 20,000 feet where you are benevolently, curiously, watching the snaking lineups at Ellis Island work their way through the entry gates. Get grounded again, into your reality, into this here and now. To solve the puzzle, to finish the game, what do you need to give them? What do you need to show? What do you have? What are the things they will care about? Not you, them, the authorities sitting expressionless behind a computer, or sorting through piles of file folders. Do this for them. You, and how you feel about it all, can come later.

So, let's begin. Let's put aside the extended immigration files except for that one page of a document that noted my great-grandmother's name change, which slashed the apple from the orchard in Waldapfel and left a nondescript forest that was not too hard to pronounce for anglicized tongues. Let's put aside everything I had found that represented my grandfather's journey as an economic migrant because, without being the "persecuted ancestor," he is just one link in the chain proving a connection. His story is not the focus of this round, even if I had wanted it to be. Her story, his mother's story, is the only one that matters in depth here and now.

For my great-grandmother, we had quite a lot on hand, just from official documents that were in the box and my online searches, which included scanned files in the public databases. We had her Austrian passport issued in 1938, we had the ship manifest with her arrival in New York on June 20 of that year, and we had the naturalization documents that started her way to ensuring permanence on this side of the Atlantic as soon as they were reasonably able to begin that final process. For my grandfather, we did not have anything that stated who his parents were on hand. But we could get his death certificate, and we could probably request his marriage license: The 1942 registry of New York City marriage licenses had been scanned online, with the document number, if not the document itself. His parents' names should be listed on those documents. For my mother, we had a short version of her marriage license. But we could get her birth certificate, and we could get a long version of her marriage license, both of which would have my grandparents' names as well. I had all my documents, with my parents listed, although my birth certificate was on half a sheet of paper and did not seem to have all the details that a birth certificate on a full sheet of paper would have and the Austrian authorities might want. I made a mental note to reorder it while we're going through everything else. It should not take too long to arrive. It was not so long ago, even if my age is starting to show.

Checking further into the details and reading the fine print, there was no official translation to German required for English-language documents even though they were going to a German-speaking country where English was not an official language. I breathed a deep sigh of relief. No official translations meant one fewer layer to the documents, which meant less time and money. Apostilles were only officially required for the applicants themselves, not for any of the documents designed to prove a background point or support an 80-year-old connection.

All right, all right, all right. Calm down. Breathe. Assess it realistically. This felt reasonable. This felt manageable. This felt doable. I knew I could manage it at this point. Everything was out there; I just needed to request it and get it delivered so I could assemble the full file and send it along to the Austrians. First, where were our American documents all from? Which states? Massachusetts and New York.

I was piecing all this together from my parents' house, from my childhood bedroom, during that fall and winter that was the worst of the COVID pandemic. This was before vaccines became available for everyone, before life began haltingly to return to a kind of normal. It was two steps forward and one step back. I was piecing all of this together as overly enthusiastic predictions about vaccine efficacy gave way to new variants, continued fear, and ongoing isolation, with a few blips of normalcy as caseloads went down before they bounced back up like a pogo stick. It was a strange time that was anything but normal when I had the bandwidth, energy, and focus to pull all of this together.

Under normal circumstances, I might have taken a road trip to request the different documents in Massachusetts and eastern New York, which share a small border. I would have justified the concentrated time and effort it would take to revisit all these different places where momentous events in my family's American story had taken place by telling myself there would be less waiting, and maybe I could corral a family member or friend to come with me. It could be an adventure down memory lane, taking detours and diversions off the interstate to see what was still around from the different times when we had populated these locales.

I thought of a loop, starting from that condominium in suburban Boston where all of this activity was taking shape, and heading out west, an hour down the scenic state highway I knew so well from years of going to see my brother at college, and then taking trips into the countryside as hiking became my all-consuming hobby. My mother was born in Greenfield, Massachusetts, when her parents were living there during one of their extended exoduses and my grandfather was putting all of his chips into a factory that made television cabinets. That was where her birth certificate was housed. From Greenfield, we would go south on Interstate 91, through central

Massachusetts's Pioneer Valley, and then cut west to New York's Hudson Highlands, where I was born and spent the first years of my childhood. My birth certificate would be there in Middletown. Then we would swing even further south, making stops in three different boroughs of New York City – Manhattan, Brooklyn, and the Bronx – to collect a variety of birth, death, and marriage certificates. Finally, we would loop back northeast, making the stops on Interstate 84 that we used to make going back and forth between the condominium in suburban Boston and my grandparents' apartment, where this journey began. I thought I could make the journey last a week, and in my mind, it would be a lovely week.

During the worst winter of the pandemic, making this kind of trip was an impossibility, pure fantasy. It was like building a castle on Mars. None of the town or city municipal offices that would issue these documents were open to the public. Everything was done by phone and mail to prevent unnecessary exposure to coronavirus. They were necessary public health measures but exasperating and exhausting when I wanted to compile these documents as quickly as possible and didn't trust local administrators to be expedient or efficient in issuing them.

I worried at every step of the process. I worried whether the requests would get there. I worried about how long processing would take. I worried that once they were processed, they would get lost in the mail on the way back to me. I worried about all the things I could not control that being able to go to these offices would have circumvented. But there were no other options in the short term. It was mail and phone. The other option was to wait until some unclear moment in the distant future, potentially years, or never, when things would reopen to the public.

It turned out that my fears and paranoia were completely unfounded for the Massachusetts documents. I felt a bit guilty afterward for doubting the local gatekeepers. Massachusetts was so easy, even during the pandemic, even while keeping a physical distance from strangers, without my being able to exert an immediate urgency by being in front of a recordkeeper and watching them physically go back to an archive or storeroom to look up the record on request.

I learned that in Massachusetts, if you know what type of document you're requesting and are authorized to do so because of your relationship to the person whose document you are requesting, you can order vital records online directly from any town or city on a website. That's it. Nothing special. Just as easy as ordering dinner from an online takeout menu. Just as intuitive as ordering anything else over the internet. We ordered my mother's birth certificate and my grandfather's death certificate online from two different towns in less than an hour. They both arrived at the house in less than a week. From there, it was also easy to mail the certified copies of these documents to Boston rather than going into the city for a same-day apostille at the Massachusetts Department of State. Those documents were deposited at the post office with a self-addressed, stamped return envelope and a check for $12 US. Considering how much parking cost, sending it by mail was certainly much cheaper than driving over. The good people at the Commonwealth of Massachusetts did their part, and everything was doubly certified and back to us in two weeks. It was too good to be true. All governments should be so easy to work with.

New York, however, was another story. New York City is treated differently from the rest of the large, sprawling state, the fourth largest by population in the United States, where the steps vary depending on which county the document was issued in.

For New York City, the pandemic probably made the process worse. It was next to impossible to ask for help beyond what was published on websites. Getting people on the phone was a nightmare. I wanted some reassurance at least that I was filling out complex forms correctly the first time, that I would not have to redo, re-request, re-pay. I did not get it. There was no easy way to work through the process, to reduce the stress and aggravation for everyone involved – especially myself.

I braced myself for the bureaucratic equivalent of pulling teeth. Five documents had been issued in New York City and State that needed to be correct in the eyes of the Austrians come hell or high water: my great-grandmother's death certificate, my grandparents' and parents' marriage licenses, my brother's birth certificate, and my birth certificate. There was no turning back or alternative if I wanted this to happen. I would have to work with New York from afar.

The same remote request was necessary for all the towns, cities, counties, and jurisdictions. Depending on the city or county, it was either a paper or an online request. Some needed to be notarized, others needed different types of sworn authorizations. In many cases, personal checks for issuing documents were not accepted, only certified checks or money orders, with an underlying tone of "We do not trust you, so pay up first or do not bother," without any assurance I would get the document I needed.

In New York, as in other larger states like California and Texas, after a document is issued (whether in weeks or months), the path to an apostille goes through two additional steps that are slightly less nefarious but also present potential landmines. The next step is mailing it to the county seat of the county it was issued in to have it certified unless it already has a preemptive extra exemplification. Or maybe even if it does; I cannot remember at this point. The final step, once you get the certified document back, is mailing it to Albany, the state capital, where the apostille is issued. Not simple, not streamlined, not an ordeal anyone would voluntarily undertake considering the painstaking detail.

Those were just the broad strokes for New York State, writ large. New York City presented a whole other set of layers sprawling below and alongside the broader state bureaucracy. The tentacles of a completely unwieldy mass of paperwork and approvals stretched out and curved around in unexpected directions that you would not be able to swat away or plan for. Unless, of course, you had already become mired in the depths and managed to emerge from the churning dross with that sought-after paper plus an extra set with raised seals and formal signatures duly affixed, clutched triumphantly so nobody can take them away.

I still do not think I completely understood all the various combinations and permutations of bureaucracy one might have to go through. I just knew what I had already experienced, which was different for someone else dealing with other parts of New York City, across the river in New Jersey, or anything other than the specific path. I understood that New York City truly is a world unto itself. There is no other way to conceive of it.

Each borough in New York City is its own county. Each county issues and stores its own documents. Eventually, some of these documents are transferred to central repositories or archives for the city as a theoretical, if not practical, unified whole. When that transfer happens is unclear. Other unclear elements of this bureaucratic hodgepodge of activity include which documents are transferred or how frequently. The websites and subsites are disjointed. Phone numbers to call for clarification are disconnected or go unanswered.

Seeing how complicated this truly was, I tried to keep New York City to the minimum possible documents. Great-grandmother: death certificate – Manhattan, New York County. Grandfather: marriage license – Brooklyn, King's County. Mother: marriage license – Manhattan, New York County. All of these documents were requested from different bureaucratic entities within the same "city," with a different process to get an official copy and a different type of additional certification necessary.

I must have been in a quasi-fugue state while navigating these processes because to this day I have no acute memory of working through them. I did, but I just cannot remember how. And now, summarizing what happened, reliving the paperwork flying back and forth, up and down, side to side, I find myself entering a sort of confusion and panic. I had done complex immigration paperwork processes for myself but never like this. Never the combination of archival research, hoping to get lucky with online databases while at the same time going into the black hole of document requests and hoping things would get where I needed them to be. From the outside, it was orderly. From the inside, I felt the swirling chaos of bureaucracy upon bureaucracy upon bureaucracy. Kafka would either have been proud or horrified. Maybe both.

The whole process felt like I was flying blind and hoping that somewhere, deep in some office, my weeks-old request would not fall behind a furnace or into a shredder or be denied on a technicality. Am I filling out the form the right way? How long does an envelope with a request sit around before someone gets around to opening it? Will these documents arrive how Austria needs them? Am I eligible to make the request? Does it have to come from my mother? How long is all of this going to take? For a while, it seemed like it would never end.

But it did end. Sometimes I wonder if I am just so stubbornly pig-headed, a personification of a dog with a bone that it won't give up, that what may be overwhelming for someone else is manageable for me. It was following steps one by one and abiding by the rules of the game as laid out but also adapting as things changed and evolved with each new layer that I scavenged and unearthed. And when the game seemed to stall, calling every so often. If I was lucky and someone picked up, I would have the good fortune of getting to speak to a harried bureaucrat from the City of New York.

They were all, without exception, flustered and stressed: understaffed and underappreciated, running in a million directions trying to deal with remote requests without the ease of in-person communication. Despite, or perhaps because of, this palpable frustration, they always somehow made the time to be on the phone kindly chatting away with a stranger about how much work they were dealing with. Ten to 15 minutes of sympathetically listening and comforting interjections from my end before I could ask my question. I could not really get a word in edgewise, but I did not necessarily mind being nice and letting them vent. That is also how I had learned to play the game, to accept their frazzled bureaucratic stress, in the hope that it meant my request would be looked on favorably whenever they got around to it.

I guess my sympathetic strategy paid off even if I could not quite believe it when we had everything we needed. New York City in all of its myriad manifestations of mangled offices and recordkeeping came through with all the necessary documents and certifications. The state came through with the rest.

Finally, last but certainly not least, was the federal stage. We did not need to apostille any of the archival documents. We did not even need certified copies of the immigration files. Those were nice to have in the file as supporting evidence for when my great-grandmother fled Vienna and arrived in New York. But they did not seem to affect the petitions themselves since we had the original 1938 passports, which provided all the information the Austrians needed. No, the only federal documents that required any additional verification were the FBI criminal background checks and apostilles, only for those of us directly applying.

These background checks were also completely new to me. Once, years before, I had requested a local background check at the state level to see what the process would be like if someone asked for it in my travels, in my visa applications. At the time, I was a student, so it was free – and easy – at the local police station. It turns out I was overprepared since no authority had ever asked me for a background check during any of these processes.

Knowing the background checks and apostille would come from different parts of the US federal government, I felt another wave of needing to brace myself before I even got started. Yet again, the unknown bureaucratic tubes started to snake around my neck, with a dread that it might even be many times worse and more sprawling than New York City despite the public reassurances that it could all be taken care of easily.

But it did work somehow. It turned out that the FBI has an agreement for background check fingerprinting with some post offices, so all you need to do if you're close enough to one of those centers is fill out a preorder background check form online, select the fingerprint scanning location you want, and get fingerprinted. After the fingerprints are taken, they are automatically checked against a national database managed by the FBI. Within minutes, there is a response in your inbox with an attached letter that includes information about whatever they have in their files on you. If there is nothing, you're all clear and can move on to the next step. That is it. Then you print out the letter and the correct apostille request form with a check for $20 and away it goes to an office just outside of Washington.

As luck would have it, that last part, the final push for the federal apostille, took the longest of any individual request, confirmation, or certification – about five months. If I had known it would have taken so long, I would have done everything I could to get myself to Washington to the same-day window they have at a Department of State office for these kinds of things, for those obsessive and desperate souls like me who just want to get it done. But again, during the worst of the pandemic, it was a literal impossibility. There was no way to show up at a same-day document authentication window because it was closed. So there was nothing to do other than wait and wait and wait. During those five months, I kept telling myself that, in a worst-case scenario, I could just resend it with another check for the processing fees if they had lost it.

To make what has become a long story short, with everything – all the back and forth, all the certified documents, all the tracked and registered mail, all the self-addressed and prepaid return envelopes, and all the checking the mailbox eagerly to see if something would magically appear – we finally had complete and correct applications packets as per the Austrian foreign ministry's website, and the emails we'd received from a foreign service officer at the Austrian Consulate in New York City. It all fell into place about six months and $250 after we'd started. Which was worth it, since the result would be this priceless, unique connection to the past, that we never thought would have been possible.

Sending the full package away to the Austrian Consulate in New York, which included my mother's application and my own, with our joint documentation, was both terrifying and empowering at the same time. Terrifying because it had been such a long and draining process during the isolation of the pandemic. It was time to send it away, though, because it was coming to a point where I had done all I could. First came a new understanding of my family, where they had come from, and what they had suffered through. Then came pursuing all the different types of documents, all remotely, plodding along with dogged determination and absurd attention to detail, not knowing if I was doing it correctly but doing what people told me regardless and hoping it would all work out. I endured the months of cold, frigid uncertainty and silence, the pandemic seeping through and permeating all parts of the process with a bittersweet tinge. Within all that, I exerted the control, force, and focus to keep moving things along. Sending it all away, I would no longer be in control.

It was empowering, though, because sometimes when I was by myself thinking about it, looking through the old pictures again and again, thumbing through the old passports, I was able to relax and give myself a half-smile of satisfaction. I could give myself a small pat on the back when nobody was looking. To start, there was everything I discovered in less than a year about my family. Then, there was all I learned about the work it takes to pull a descendance citizenship application like this together, all the historical records, combined with all the bureaucratic wrangling. I was proud of myself for having done it, having given it the best of my abilities, shot my best shot when never in a million years would I have thought I could have a chance at a European passport. At least, I would know I had tried. It was, without a doubt, time to let it all go, put our file out on the next part of its journey, and let the fates, along with a new set of unknown bureaucrats on the other side of the Atlantic Ocean, decide.

XIII. WAITING

In the best of circumstances, I am not the most patient person. In fact, I am actively impatient. When I decide I want to do something and try to make it happen, I want to see results as soon as possible. I want it to be done, and I want to be able to move on, checking that item off the list, one less thing to track on a list that ultimately never ends.

I want to think that I can expediently avoid the tedium and uncertainty of that in-between zone when you want something to happen but it is slowly inching its way through the tubes of destiny deciding whether it will happen. I want to think that, with my effort, good humor, organization, and all these other great skill sets I have developed and honed over the years, things will move and happen.

Of course, with age and experience, I have gotten a little more patient. There is no other choice when you're working with timelines you have no control over, as is often the case despite a human desire to think otherwise. I do not check my email compulsively after I send something out anymore; I do not expect an immediate response. Sometimes it takes a while to get the response you're hoping for, and nothing you can do will change that. I know worthwhile things take time, and I know patience is essential. I know that proverbial days of watching the sunrise and sunset without things working out are necessary, if hard. I know that my urgency is not someone else's.

Trying to be patient still brings me anxiety, and I do what I can to assuage that. I move my body – whether on a mat or up a mountain. I put away my electronics so they're not keeping me tethered to someone else's priorities for what I do with my time. I get out so I can see something else, stop running things around on the hamster wheel in my head, allow the waves of focus to ebb and flow, or go slack and completely turn off, disconnecting for the time being.

We all get pulled back eventually. The rope that tethers us to that thing we want – whatever it may be – tenses back up and we're drawn to attention. There is an email asking for more information: Do you have it, and can you send it over when you get a chance? There is a request to confirm something: You must quickly say yes and click a button so you're not the reason things aren't advancing and the blame cannot be placed on you. There's the jolt back to attention.

As I waited impatiently, mentally measuring the weeks and months since I had last heard a response from anyone, curious about whether it would be too soon to follow up again, knowing that if I was asking myself that question it probably was too soon, there were a couple of external lampposts to guide the way, providing hope that we were on the right track and that the waiting would not come to naught.

I started researching in October 2020, and we submitted our documentation in May 2021. Our claims were sent on by the consulate to Vienna in early June. As I was waiting for everything to come back, from the consulate, waiting for confirmation, waiting for the real waiting to begin, I learned that the Austrians had inaugurated a new Holocaust memorial in Vienna back in the fall of 2020. Back when I was doing my own research in the family box and with what I could find online. The new memorial listed the 65,000 Austrians who had been murdered by the Nazi regime, in alphabetical order on stone slabs for all the world to see. They had recorded the inauguration and posted it online. I watched the first half or so on YouTube with a translation into English. The event was held in a COVID-appropriate tent, with social distancing, masking, and everything else that the COVID-conscious world required, a few weeks before the whole country unexpectedly went back into lockdown before Christmas 2020.

From what I watched from afar, it was a lot and it was intense, even with translation. To me, it felt like the Austrian officials speaking were trying hard, so very hard, to be conscientious about what their grandparents, what their great-grandparents, had unleashed. They were repenting in a way for things that they did not know they had to repent for when they were younger, but they were belatedly assuming the mantle despite being unsure of its sizing and if it would fit. They were beating themselves on their chests lightly, though not the intense and bloody self-flagellation that some Catholics still do during Holy Week. But despite the intensity and uncertainty, it felt like too little, too late. I could not quite place my finger on why. They were there, doing their best. Who was I to criticize that finally, for once, they were putting a name, many thousands of names, on what they had done wrong?

After I could not watch anymore, I looked up the project online, these stone slabs that had taken 80 years to come to fruition just a ten-minute walk from the old Freud house, inscribed in permanence with masses of names of the women, children, and men who were of this place and had lost their lives by not running from danger, not running from their neighbors, not assuming the worst would happen. I went to the database from which those names had been pulled. I looked up the Waldapfels, the ones who had been left behind, the ones who could not get out. None of them had lived at Klopstockgasse 29 anymore, but a number had still been scattered throughout the city. Almost all of them were old – thought of as even older back then when the generations were born closer together and people lived shorter lives. They were older than Irma Waldapfel when she fled; some of these Waldapfels were born in the 1850s and 1860s. I was alone, but I shook my head, speechless at seeing this new, hard, expanded reality.

At least the Austrians were not trying to hide it anymore. At least it was all out there for anyone who might stumble across it while walking down that particular street. A monumental version of the Stolpersteine [stumbling stone] metal plate markers on sidewalks that people come across in Vienna and other cities that commemorate the people who used to live there and whose lives as they knew them were forced to end.

It was out there in public even during COVID delays, hiatuses, and unanticipated lockdowns when people were not allowed to go into the office and documents to be verified languished on unvisited desktops. Even in the stop-and-go of different confirmations being requested over email, of wondering how difficult it could be to substantiate information that was so clearly laid out. Even within all that personal frustration and annoyance, they were putting themselves out there, and finally, publicly, recognizing that their parents, grandparents, and great-grandparents had been monsters to their friends and neighbors.

So if they were not trying to hide it anymore, maybe my family should not hide, either. Maybe this would be an opportunity to put a version of our story out there in a way that nobody felt comfortable doing before because the future was more hopeful and more important than the past. Even though, conversely, you also need to know your past to better understand your present and move into your future with confidence. Maybe part of this process could be putting some of what was in that box out there for all to see.

At first, I had been very utilitarian with those old letters. I had already taken pictures of them and interacted with them in terms of our Austrian citizenship application directly, nothing more. I thought there might be something in the letters that laid out my family's reality in 1937 and 1938 so the Austrians would have even more evidence that my family had been persecuted and victimized. There was nothing there, though, not in that sense. The letters were mostly mundane, about household routines and family gossip. But, as my friend from Germany had mentioned, many self-censored out of fear of the letters being intercepted by authorities. It did not mean they were unafraid as the danger increased. So, without any reason to dig any deeper, I put the letters back into the box, organized by date as best I could ascertain.

I checked the box. The letters were still there. If a detective had put a hair on the folder, like in an old mystery novel, it still would have been there. Nobody had touched them since I put them back. Maybe the letters would fit with some other things, other places, and woven together with other people and their experiences, re-create the world that was left behind. I started looking online, thinking about where this would fit. Would it be something about the Jewish experience? Or about the Holocaust itself?

Nobody had ever framed what happened to my great-grandmother as being a victim or survivor of the Holocaust. That felt extreme. She was lucky. She had gotten out. She had avoided the worst and rebuilt her life. But the Jewish museums also seemed insufficient. It was not about a snapshot of their lives as part of a society that was destroyed and took decades to begin rebuilding the ashes. It was about understanding the strangely dynamic nature of what they had gone through, events they never expected yet responded to and grew from as best they knew how. That was it, in its simplest form, crystallized in my mind. The pivots, not choices, they were forced to make, and the circumstances to which they had to adapt.

I finally, hopefully, but reluctantly, reached out to the US Holocaust Memorial Museum. I wanted the box to stay in the United States because this is where my great-grandmother and her children chose to become citizens and flourished. This is where my family, such as it is, has its roots now. If such personal things were going to go anywhere, they at least should stay in the United States. That seemed right. They also seemed to have better infrastructure, more robust scholarship. It seemed if things got sent there, there was more of a chance they would have life breathed back into them, not be confined to a dusty archive. Maybe they would be translated. Maybe they would serve a purpose. Maybe the voices of those letter-writers would reach beyond the grave.

I wrote, at first, to the head of the research department. I was grasping at straws a bit and thought these letters, coming from the type of people about whom history is rarely written, would be interesting. The kind of regular, working-class people who are often forgotten as the historical narrative focuses on the more extreme, wealthier parts of society. History often lacks a narrative about regular people just trying to get by, perhaps integrated into some fancy aspects of their societies but mostly just adjacent, watching out the window. Now that I knew that my family members were just regular people, I wanted to honor who they were, how hard they worked, and the ordinary lives they lived in very difficult times.

> I am writing because I have recently been organizing family documents from my great-grandmother and great-aunt's flight from Nazi-occupied Vienna in June 1938, so that my mother and I can apply for Austrian nationality as direct descendants of persons persecuted by the Nazi regime per recent changes to Austrian citizenship law.
>
> We are in possession of the passports and exit visas of my great-grandmother as well as a series of letters from 1937-8 between the two of them and relatives in the US, in addition to some era-specific family pictures and documents and letters from people who I assume have some kind of family relation. My mother came into possession of these items that may be of historical interest through a death in the family ...

He was nice and replied, and although it was the wrong department, he did point me in the right direction. The right direction was his colleague, a woman whose job as a curator seemed to include outreach to increase the museum's collections as direct victims continued to pass away and more and more of these types of relics were accidentally tossed out with the trash and destroyed. We exchanged some emails and arranged for a brief call by way of introduction. I mentioned that my mother would need to be there because ultimately the documents were hers. And any formal donation would, of course, need to come from her.

We had an initial video call with her. We sat side by side at the dining room table, with our backs to the teak credenza, inches from where the box had laid dormant all those years, with a laptop open on the dining room table in front of us. The curator was patient and asked many questions about the family and everything that had happened, taking notes as my mother talked and I interjected with the historical nuances I had uncovered that I thought might be relevant. My mother did not seem bothered by these interjections and I was glad to have something to contribute, something with extra value.

It was comforting to know that when we were ready, there would be a place for these letters, documents, and whatever else we wanted to include. At the museum. Preserved, archived, scanned, accessible to anyone who might be going down that rabbit hole. It is something a bit otherworldly to realize that what you may have pushed back into a corner or box for so long might have real value, that professionals who determine what might be included in an on-the-record, authoritative treasure trove think should be kept with them. It put my mother at ease, and when we had a second call a few weeks later, the donation was set.

The letters and pictures were fine; there was no problem with a donation to what we were told would be called the Waldapfel family papers. I had scanned and shared them so we could always look back on them. We had digital versions of everything we could intuitively understand, everything we could feel just from the visuals.

But the passports, no. The passports would stay. The passports and the small leather file folder where they fit perfectly would be that tactile thing we could always pull out of a drawer to feel the reality of what they had lived through before, during, and after that week-and-a-half-long journey to the US. When we wanted to, if we wanted to. We would keep those as the unique things that began this whole process in the first place. We would have them as long as we wanted.

So in the middle of waiting, after Austria had taken possession of our file and there was nothing we could do any longer on that front, we donated those letters that we could not read, those photographs that opened another world that no longer exists. It did not seem fair to have them sitting in a box, shunted aside indefinitely, locked up, beyond the grasp of people working to reconstruct those stories. The US Holocaust Memorial Museum was the right place. The US had granted the Walds the ability to live out the rest of their lives in a way they could not where they came from. They had become proud Americans in that deeply spiritual way that the United States allows so many to do and, as far as I am aware, died with no regrets about their forced journey.

I had been brought up to just get on with things, not to make a fuss about them at the expense of moving along, moving out, moving up. As an adult, I had adapted this ethos as something akin to a practical disassociation that did not let my emotions get in the way of what I was trying to achieve, the finish line somewhere way out there. So through most of this coming to terms with the reality of what happened, I tried not to think about it too much. The few times I had personalized things, it all felt too overwhelming. Whatever I allowed myself to feel came in waves, crashing on top of me and pulling me under. The feelings felt too big to manage, as though they would tear down the door and attack me the minute I let them.

But the donation, this process, made me understand more deeply that this was bigger than just trying to feel like myself, like an ordinary person working through an extraordinary box of unremembered memories. It is all too personal a thing to keep at arm's length; like trying not to cry at your own wedding, it is simply impossible. I wondered to myself what I would have done had I been in their shoes. What I would have packed, what I would have tried to save. How I would have made peace with what had been forced on me.

They never considered themselves victims, as far as I knew. The more I thought about it, the more convinced I became that it was a matter of pride. If you are not a victim, then they do not hold anything over you. If you are not a victim, you can choose to tell yourself whatever you want. You can tell your story in a way that makes you feel however you need to about what happened, all those things you could not control as it was going on.

But whatever had happened to them, and however they felt about what they were subject to, it was all over now. And what mattered was how we felt, how I felt, about putting all of this together and making these donations.

I felt proud. This donation felt elevated, transcendental. Felt permanent in the way I imagine them feeling when they received positive notice that their citizenship applications in the United States had been approved and there was no fear anymore that they would have to go anywhere else. Felt floating above how I normally let myself feel about things. Felt proud of myself, proud of this project. I hoped they would be proud of me if they knew what I was doing. I hoped they would be glad that at least some of what was in the box would not be forgotten.

XIV. VALIDATION

After months of waiting, of second-guessing, of politely writing to the municipal authority of Vienna and asking if our case manager needed anything else, the official notification came very suddenly at the end of a normal weekday in early January when I was not expecting it. It was Wednesday, January 5, at the tail end of the Catholic vacation period that can stretch for nearly a month, and when, even if people are going into the office, in my experience very little gets done. I was shocked to receive an email titled "Austrian Citizenship §58c (1a) StbG; Final decision [*Bescheid*] – Anne Hand." It showed that at least some of what I had heard and internalized about slow and inefficient Austrian bureaucracy was wrong.

I thought the notification would come with a sensation of excitement and joy washing over me, knowing that the whole process had worked and that I had done it right. A clear sense of permanence that I had the right to be there. That I deserved to be there. That a successful adjudication of our case was the well-earned fruit of my labor. I had accomplished it for myself and other people, like my great-grandmother, who were never offered this chance to merge their identities and put another part of their lives back together. I expected to feel a sense of relief and happiness that I would, for the rest of my life, be a reminder both that awful things can happen and that they will happen again without a conscious effort to stop them before the seeds are planted. And, conversely, even when they happen, it is never too late to offer an olive branch of forgiveness and reunification.

But no, that is not what happened. Of course not. That would be the movie ending. In the real-life version, all I felt was shock and disbelief. I was working from home that day, wrapping up a few hours of extremely focused and tedious tasks editing a new set of online courses with my blinders on. I was finishing up the day with a review process for a colleague, the kind of thing that they ask you to do as a favor because it is so monotonous and you need another set of eyes to power through it. That was my afternoon activity, and then I did my timesheet. I was so glad to shut down the computer and call it a day. A couple of minutes later, I saw my phone blinking with a small blue light and almost did not pick it up even though technically I was still on the clock. I was so ready to be off work devices for the day and just leave the apartment.

I did pick it up, of course, expecting it to be a last-minute request for something that would have to get done first thing in the morning because my brain was fried, because that is what end-of-the-day emails usually are. The dross that people send out in corporate environments when they want to get something off their plate and onto yours when you still have a little bit of attention.

It was not that. It was an email from the same consular officer who had received our documentation the previous May, who had been rather brusque on the phone and never returned emails. I knew what the email was about from the title and because back in November someone from the office in Vienna said our file was out for a final review. But I still opened it in nervous disbelief.

We are delighted to inform you about the positive decision of the Vienna Provincial Government ...

I felt my stomach drop out from under me. A shock and nausea swept over my body, my hand released a small, unexpected tremor, and I had to put down the phone before I accidentally dropped it. It was a strange physical reaction that I was not expecting. I was surprised at my visceral response to something that, on a more intellectual and objective level, I knew would be coming. I felt myself breathing in, breathing out, trying to calm down this unconscious, autonomic response before it got the best of me. I closed my eyes for a few seconds and breathed out deeply. The shaking subsided.

At that point, a few seconds later, I texted my mother, telling her to check her email. The official notification from Austria had come in for me and likely would be in her inbox as well.

Then I read the full email.

> ... regarding your Austrian Citizenship proceedings pursuant to Article 58c (1a) Austrian Citizenship Act.
>
> Please find attached the following documents:
>
> a scan of the final decision [*Bescheid*]
>
> please check if the information (Name, DOB, POB – city/town/village) on the document is correct
>
> a letter from the Consul General
>
> Please inform us whether you would like to pick up the original documents in person at the Austrian Consulate General in New York or receive them via registered mail. If you decide to come in person, you may apply for a passport at the same time.
>
> To make an appointment, please contact us directly (do not use the online calendar). If you have any questions, please do not hesitate to contact the Austrian Consulate General.

My partner was in another room of our apartment working as well. I called him over to show him, to make sure I was not misreading or misunderstanding. I was not. It was all there, clear as day, no room for questions. "How do you feel?" he asked, knowing full well the process that had taken up so much room in my psyche for so long, using up so much existential energy. I did not know how to answer that question. I felt calm now that I had stopped shaking. It did not feel real, so how could I feel anything?

My mother checked her email and told me she had received it as well. We did not have much to say about it. All the talking about what those people she grew up with would have thought happened before we sent the files. Now we talked about cold logistics, thinking about when would be a good time to go to Manhattan together and work through the last official step of the process. There was never a question that we would go to apply for our passports together. It seemed silly to leave it for later when that was the practical reason behind our efforts. Her vacation time would be best, in late February. We could make an overnight trip of it. At that moment, that was all we had to say.

I hung up the phone with a sense of restless, nervous anticipation. Not exactly jumping out of my skin but needing an outlet for some unsettled energy. My partner finished up his work for the day. After a little while, when things still did not feel normal and I needed to get out of the house, we went around the corner to get something to eat. We went to the little luncheonette with three tables and a counter that a family of Venezuelan refugees had been running for a few years. We went there regularly. Conversation there was light and breezy. It was the type of place where people took the time to chat, to be positive, and to make the best of extremely complicated situations just below the surface where there was no choice but to get on with it all. Now that I had a family story that echoed some of these realities, I could relate to them.

As we took the three-minute walk to the luncheonette, my partner was much more excited than I was, ebullient in his joy for me. I wanted to feel like that as opposed to the numbness that I still felt, as though I was outside my body and the notification had happened for someone else. I had expected to feel happy, and light, as though I was floating when the news came in. It had been such a process to dig into a world that, on some unspoken level, people had felt for many years was better forgotten. And then the waiting, the not knowing, the being available in case this would be the day they would email with a resolution or the time they asked a question and I would not be able to respond quickly, delaying the whole thing. It was hard to believe the process was over. I would soon have to fill out forms differently, as a dual national, without really knowing what those implications would be, or who would even care.

When we sat down at the only empty table at the restaurant, which was busy even though not a regular mealtime, it still did not feel normal. When my partner proudly told the owners that the paperwork had ended, that I was now European, Austrian, I did not know what to say. He had told them before. They were intrigued with the whole concept, that Europe had once been so complicated as to eject millions of its own and some of the countries wanted to make amends. They knew what it felt like from their own experience.

I hid a little and shied away because I knew they were in the middle of their own nefariously bureaucratic immigration process. They were glad to be out of Venezuela, of course, but concerned with their own place in the world until they had certainty they could stay. We had already talked about my application and how you never know what will happen, the twists and turns that life takes you on. They and millions of other Venezuelans who had fled a country that had been prosperous when they were younger and been in decline for so long certainly knew that well enough.

They were excited for me, of course. What did it mean? Well, nothing, really, in the short term. I would have to figure out the documentation piece, how to finalize everything and get a passport. There were still a few more steps to go. Oh, all right, it was still good that the black box of administrative bureaucracy was done and it was all approved. There was not a lot more to say about it, so the conversation moved on to other, more mundane matters. I was grateful for that. I was grateful that the curiosity was muted because I did not know what to say. I did not know how to feel. I did not know why I felt so confused when this seemed like something I wanted, that I had worked toward for a long time.

I let it sit for a few days and got back to work. Something I am very good at is letting change marinate in itself, allowing myself time to feel what I need to feel and begin to put words with the feelings, like slowly putting together a mental puzzle that allows me to express my true emotions. This was a big change, though, bigger than any I had felt in recent years. A few days later, it still did not feel normal.

I tried to do physical things to make this change seem more present. I went back to the luncheonette as it was opening, bringing some thick pieces of sweetly tangy apple strudel we had bought from a neighborhood bakery to eat at home, to taste and share more of the flavors that are strongly associated with snow and the mountains. To feel the connection in a more visceral way than just getting an email with a notice that some documents had been approved. To share it with people who had been kind throughout the process. They received the sweet bread with curiosity. They appreciated the gesture, but the flavors were different for them, so they did not feel them as deeply as I did. They were nice flavors, homey but different. I probably would not react the same way to foods that opened the door to home to them.

I tried to normalize the news for myself and spread the word gradually, focusing on people who I thought might be interested. Maybe by telling other people who had been involved at one point or another, it would feel more real. Over the following week, as I internalized the news, I reached out to everyone with whom I had remembered even peripherally talking about the process. Lots of European friends, colleagues, and former colleagues who were supportive, especially the Germans. American and Canadian friends who had already undergone their own citizenship processes, who understood how exciting and weird, somewhat surreal, it is to see yourself from different angles. Lots of people here and there who had been part of the process, those I had talked about it with who had a similar international bent, who had their own immigration stories, who had their own ways of moving through the world in ways not everyone can understand.

Everyone was happy, of course, and glad to hear of the resolution. Excited about the possibilities it implied, and the ease with which I could work and live in Europe. For me, at my stage in life, in the relative stability that I had but did not take for granted, those assumptions had always been hypothetical, more like "nice to haves." For other people, though, they were not hypotheticals. Out came immediate questions based on assumptions about an impending move date that had never been on the table, had never been part of my thought process. It was surprising to hear that so many people thought I would move to Europe immediately upon receiving a passport from the European Union even though my entire career and life was focused on the Americas. I wondered if I had ever given an impression that I was unhappy with my life and wanted that kind of momentous change even though I strongly believe that you cannot run away from yourself.

There were general well wishes and good tidings and invitations to stay with friends in Paris, Berlin, and other locales where people with internationalist leanings live. Some people expressed surprise at the resolution, especially since the process had been so successful in such a relatively short amount of time. Some reminisced about their own experiences, with passports being held up for months in other immigration processes and not being able to leave the country while those bureaucratic machinations went on. My process was all so easy.

And that was that – the neatly closed ending that seemed so straightforward. The petition was approved, and we would soon finish the paperwork and be Austrian, again. Pick up the mantle again where my great-grandmother and grandfather had left it behind. But if it was that straightforward, why did I still feel unsettled? Why did ruminations about what it all meant keep going in circles in my head? Why did I want to keep talking about it? Why did I want to bore my friends to tears, continuing to analyze what all this meant when there was nothing new left to say? Why could I not just accept that it was over and move on, now with more, better access to a world that had only been peripherally open before?

Precisely because it was not over, not in a way that would bring me the peace to counter all that my research had unearthed. The technical part was over, but I could not know what it all would mean. Not so soon, not in my soul when it had been so many years, so many generations in the making. Knowing that the door was open was one thing, but walking through it and into this unknown facet of the world was something else entirely. It would require time and energy that I did not have at that point when the focus had been on getting a successful response.

Truly assimilating this new part of my identity, of defining who I was in the world, would require a focus that I could not have until I was able to take the time to truly begin to experience what it might mean. Until things were resolved and there were no more bureaucratic hurdles to jump over. Those types of tremendous changes that shift us into a new normal rarely happen overnight or immediately. I would have to wait and see what being a new Austrian would look like. I would have to be patient with myself, and the unknown that was yet to come, whatever it would end up becoming.

XV. COMMEMORATION

My mother and I reached out to our consular officer in New York who had previously been sparse with his responses and got a bit more information from him about wrapping up the citizenship process. He gave us detailed information about what we'd need to bring to the appointment to sign off on the last paperwork, apply for passports, and get other new documentation needed for recognition as Austrians anywhere in the world. We made an appointment when my mother would be on vacation from her job as a high school teacher in a few weeks. We made hotel reservations in midtown Manhattan so we could walk between Penn Station, the hotel, and the Austrian consulate. It would be amazing to be able to get around New York City without the subway or a cab. The same New York City where, for years, nobody would have dreamed of staying in a hotel, even if it was more convenient to the business at hand, because "Why would you waste your money on that when you could stay with family?"

Of all the addresses my family members had in New York City over the years – in all the boroughs except for Staten Island – the closest to the consulate was where my great-grandmother had died. It was, at the time she lived there, a stately apartment in a rent-controlled building close to Carnegie Hall. She and her two unmarried daughters, my great-aunts Valerie and Karla, lived there for years until she passed away at home. The building at 161 West 54th Street is a comfortable, easy, 20-minute walk to 31 East 69th Street, the location of the Austrian Consulate. The stroll cuts through the southeastern corner of Central Park on well-marked paths, past well-known tourist sites like the zoo and the ice-skating rink, and weaves through backdrops that have been captured in countless films and photographs since Manhattan became the backdrop for a certain type of globalized cosmopolitanism. For someone who has never been there before, it is a strange feeling since they have been exposed to these places frequently if they consume any type of American popular culture.

I wondered if my great-grandmother and great-aunts had ever made that walk themselves to wrap up any unfinished business with the new Austrian government after the war. In 1957, when they applied for restitution for the liquor store and bar from the national fund, who was the one to manage the paperwork and request? That was nearly 20 years after Irma and Karla had arrived and nearly 35 years after Valerie made the long sea journey by herself. Hopefully, any residual fear had passed. They were all naturalized US citizens at that point, had lost any claim as far as they were aware to Austrian nationality. They were really, truly, unequivocally American. There should not have been anything to worry about. Or was there still something that festered within them that they preferred not to pick at like a scab? Something that they knew they would rather not unearth? Had they avoided going there, to that physical manifestation of the place they had fled and still existed in their new lives? Maybe they sent someone else, a lawyer, someone else with a power of attorney, or a courier to take that physically easy but mentally taxing stroll and drop everything off for them. I would never know.

We had no family left to stay with, not in the city proper, not close enough to midtown Manhattan to make it worthwhile for a quick visit. We booked our room on the east side of midtown between

Grand Central Station and the United Nations with my father's hotel points. We anticipated the journey, which took on an exciting life of its own. Now that it was happening, my mother excitedly mentioned that she'd always wanted to go on a business trip to New York, taking the train and staying in a hotel.

We certainly had business to attend to. This was the closest we would get to a business trip together in the foreseeable future. It was now late winter 2022, nearly two years after the pandemic had started and a year since I had finished my family research; that winter's Omicron wave was beginning to wane, although it was still difficult to know in advance where we would have unfettered access to things. We coordinated what we should do in the placid suburbs before embarking on the journey. Things like taking new passport pictures to Austrian specifications and making copies of forms that were easier to get done without the throngs of undulating, grumpy people and the long lines of Manhattan. Other things would be better left to when we were there, like actually completing the forms, since they were left untranslated in a German that neither of us could read particularly well. Hopefully, the consular officer could help us there. With great excitement, we talked up the food we would eat for the four meals that we would be there for, especially the simple, greasy pizza and smoky, salty delicatessen meat that doesn't taste the same anywhere else in the world.

We decided that, in addition to being an integral part of my mother's ideal business trip, the easiest transportation option would be the train. It had been years since I last took that four-hour Amtrak ride from the Boston suburbs to midtown Manhattan, a trip that always felt grand and sophisticated with so much to see as the train wove its way from Massachusetts to Rhode Island to Connecticut to New York, with the coastal postcard landscape visible on most of the journey ebbing and flowing. It was always somewhat expensive, a luxury compared to the tedious task of driving a car full of people, and felt fancy. It was the way my grandmother came to visit after my grandfather had passed away and she was still well enough to travel on her own. It was always a special, more comfortable, less stressful way to travel. I bought the nonrefundable tickets. We were going on my mother's long-awaited business trip.

I did our bureaucratic homework. I read up on the identity documents we could request and the forms we needed to make those formal requests. I downloaded the forms, and we printed them out in triplicate. I checked the requirements for passport photos. The day before we left, we spent an hour in the closest pharmacy to my parents' house. I must have driven the poor woman working there crazy. I was so precise about having photographs as per the Austrian requirements, repeatedly asking her to retake and reprint images where our heads were slightly tilted or our ears not fully visible. It was my way of trying to prevent the unexpected, trying to avoid running around and looking for a CVS on the Upper East Side.

My mother concerned herself with more personal preparations. She made lunch to bring because who knew how expensive it would now be to buy subpar food on the train? Who knew how much prices had increased since the pandemic decimated travel over the previous year and a half? She made sure we had a few tiny bottles of vodka on hand because "would not it be nice to have a little happy hour while we were on the road? Or celebrate once we were all done?" She took some time and carefully looked through the photos we had saved, the ones that hadn't been sent to the US Holocaust Museum. She hand-picked a few to bring to the consulate, to show our consular officer, to connect him or anyone else who might have been interested to why we were there.

As with other eagerly anticipated moments that come after careful planning, the day arrived before we knew it. We were both off from work that Monday morning, excited and nervous, ready to get going and have our big adventure. My father, who was not going along for the full ride, drove us to the train station. He dropped us off well in advance and we waited around in the lobby for our midday train that would get us into Penn Station at a reasonable time, well before dinner. We had been so careful about planning, trying to foresee anything unexpected and make the trip as seamlessly stress-free as possible. We were giving ourselves plenty of time to walk to our hotel, check in while it was still light out, and then figure out a place to eat dinner.

It was Presidents' Day, the Monday of a long weekend, and most of the people in the waiting room with us looked like they were students going back to campus after a long weekend at home. I felt a nostalgia for something I had never experienced at that age – how easy, how simple, to just jump on a train for a few hours and be back in the comfortable surroundings of a permanent sense of home. No barriers, no customs checks, no boundaries that take extra time, just a flow that makes everything seem easy and integrated. Maybe I should have made my own life that much simpler for myself. No matter.

As the train came closer, we waited on the platform for it to arrive on that unseasonably mild winter day. We boarded and immediately took the empty seats closest to the door and the bathroom – more legroom, larger windows, fewer people to walk past. We settled in, immediately took out our sandwiches, and started to eat. We gazed out the window as the towns went past and the train began making all the regularly scheduled stops. I had forgotten how hypnotic train rides are. When you aren't driving, when you do not need laser-focused attention, your eyes and mind can daydream and dawdle. You can spend who knows how long watching the coastline roll past and marvel at the bridge you just went over, still standing after all these years. You can hear the countdown of the stations, checking where you are on the way to your destination, ten, five, three stops away. You can be awed at all the work on the back end, from so many people, that went into getting you where you're going.

My relationship with New York City is a bit complicated. The family I spent the most time with growing up all called it their home, but I have never personally lived there. As a child, when my grandparents were still alive, my parents, brother, and I were in and out of "the city," the only city that mattered, all the time. Crossing the George Washington Bridge into upper Manhattan and seeing Yankee

Stadium on the other side of the river was a matter of course, even if it was still a long way away from South Brooklyn, which was a second home.

As a child, spending time with my grandparents at their apartment in Trump Village (named after Fred Trump, father of Donald, the real estate developer who had built it), our life at the conflux of the Q and F elevated subway lines was mostly confined to a five-block radius. The cramped Waldbaums supermarket a block and a half toward the highway was where we lugged my grandmother's grocery cart once a week. Coney Island was a few blocks in the other direction, and Luigi's Pizzeria on Brighton Beach Avenue was my reference point for the best pizza in the world. During the summers, we would spend all day at the beach, an expanse of sand that was endless for a small child, with the acrid smell of hot dogs punctuating the salt air, and, if I was lucky, someone would get me an oversweetened, icy cold Arizona iced tea.

Sometimes, punctuating these trips, my mother and I took the subway an eternity into Manhattan if she had appointments or we wanted to go to cavernous museums. Those were always special occasions, the New York of television, not the New York of my grandparents.

That was my childhood in New York, the city where I never domiciled but was branded into my identity.

As an adult, I have never properly lived in New York City, either. I have never had to find an apartment in a market so competitive you have to make an offer immediately after a viewing. I have never had to consistently deal with the nauseating smell of rotting garbage in the summer or the frigid gusts of wind tunnels between skyscrapers in the winter. I have experienced them only in punctuated bursts. Never on a daily basis. But in many ways, this city is my cultural touchstone about how things should be. How a city works. How people live. How to get things done. How to move through the noise, the chaos, the hubbub. The kind of city where everything is there and everything is an exciting hustle, going in all directions all at once. The kind of city that is full of intensity, promise, and mystery.

I go to New York City less and less frequently these days. Life has simply taken me to other places, and the city has become tangential to who I am and what I do. The hub-and-spoke of my grandparents drawing us all back for holidays is no longer there. Friends who relocated to the city who I would have been inclined to visit have mostly found it inhospitable to their desires for creature comforts – a larger apartment, the ability to eat out without spending a full day's earnings – and have relocated closer to family or the suburbs. My work has gone remote, and even when I have clients in the city, there is no need for in-person meetings when Zoom makes everything accessible at the click of a mouse. There are fewer and fewer objective reasons for me to go and spend the time and money.

Whenever I do get a chance to go, even if only for a day or two, I am overcome with a sense of comfort and homecoming even though it has never properly been a home. The feeling is a bit confusing, I must admit. How can it feel like a home if I have never lived there? But it is the city I grew up around, and it is where my parents, and their parents, forged their lives up into the middle and upper-middle classes in their American journey. It is where I go into apartment buildings and immediately feel at home with the strange, indescribably weird odor that only exists in these behemoths, where hundreds or thousands of people live and commune and combine their body odors with poor ventilation, cheap paint, and trash. It is an odor I have never smelled anywhere else in the world. It immediately conjures up childhood memories of running down my grandparents' hallway from the elevator, past the garbage chute, to excitedly greet them after a seemingly endless car ride.

In New York City, I know where I am going, and I know how to get there on the subway. In New York City, it is never the metro, even though I have lived in places where they call it a metro. I know how to present myself, change my posture, avoid eye contact, and take off my jewelry because, well, you never know. You would never know that I have never lived there, either, because its culture is mine. It has been ingrained in me subconsciously. A latent New York accent comes out in my spoken English, the accent that my parents have and my grandparents had and could never hide even if they tried. There are people who look like me on the streets. I fit in effortlessly, but I need to make sure I have a reason to be there. A direction, a purpose to bring meaning to my stride. In New York City, you always need a purpose if you're out on the street.

It felt good to be back, as though I hadn't missed a beat. Arriving at Penn Station, we got our bearings and found an exit to go up above ground to walk. Penn Station was a place I had been through so frequently in the past, back when my father's parents were still alive in nearby Nassau County and the Long Island Railroad was the easiest way to get out to see them. It must have been at least ten years since I was last there, and there had been some changes – better lighting and new restaurants. But the wholesale renovations I had read about were greatly exaggerated.

Once we navigated the labyrinthine chasm and got above ground, we were met by construction, redirected sidewalk passages under safety awnings, and the usual confusion that comes with orienting yourself in a part of a city that, though not unfamiliar, is not part of your daily routine. We turned ourselves around a bit and began moving once we found an intersection: 34th and Seventh. We needed to get to 43rd and Second.

The landmarks were familiar, the details different. The sedate public library had sprouted new skyscrapers behind it, like scraggly tufts of facial hair on a 13-year-old boy's chin. Complex intersections where six or eight main city roads came together had new bike lanes. There were stainless-steel, weather-resistant ping-pong tables where there used to be street parking. There were an uncountable number of banking signs at corners, but not bank branches, just automated teller machines. In this initial aftermath of the worst of the pandemic, there were many empty storefronts on the straight lengths of the avenues between the smaller city blocks. As usual, people were passing by, some in idle conversation, others on a laser-focused mission for whatever they might have been doing to finish up the long weekend.

Although we were walking slowly, it did not take long to arrive – the slice of midtown Manhattan between the two train stations really is not that big. The hotel we were staying at, a Hampton Inn in a skinny tower sandwiched between two larger, squatter buildings, was just past Grand Central Station; we walked into it to take a quick look and see if anything had changed. Up until that moment, funnily enough, I hadn't quite pegged Grand Central Station as a very fancy commuter rail nexus. I had never left from there, and it hadn't clicked that there were no intercity trains that went through there. A few short blocks away, on East 43rd Street, between Second and Third Avenues, we checked into the hotel without fanfare. We signed forms to certify we did not have any COVID symptoms and got our room key. Up we went in the cramped elevator to leave our bags in the small room that was exactly what we needed, perfect for our less-than-24-hour stay, and then figured out the next segment of the day: what we were going to eat.

The next morning, we woke up early and went down for a hotel buffet breakfast. Walking through the seating area, we saw diners at each table speaking a different language – Spanish, German, Russian, Chinese, and others I could not identify. We settled in with our food in the back corner of the dining area and again talked through the paperwork we'd be filling out that day. The paperwork was just a pretext, though. It was all ready. I had made sure that everything we needed, everything they had told us to bring, was organized in folders so the photos, cash, and forms would all be easily accessible once we got to the consulate. It was as though we were steeling ourselves mentally for a precise operation yet to come, reviewing details so it would all turn out as painless and successful as possible. It was as though we needed that extra layer of mental armor to make our way up and out.

Once the topic of paperwork was thoroughly exhausted, more importantly, we talked about my grandfather again. What he would have wanted and what he might have thought of this long, strange road, which was finally culminating in this nexus of circumstances that led us to be in Manhattan with an appointment at the Austrian Consulate to make everything official. If he could have been there with us, what would he have thought, steps away from the United Nations, as we were about to move uptown toward our own entrance into having multiple passports and the ability to easily move between places? We would be Austrian again whether he wanted us to be or not. An identity he had shed as much as he could once he went on to build his new life a world away.

We finished breakfast, surprised how quickly the time had gotten away from us as we talked, and went back for second cups of coffee, and then thirds. We scurried back up to the room, quickly gathered our small overnight bags, checked out, and left about an hour before our appointment at the consulate. We began to retrace our steps from the evening before. Back over toward the United Nations, back up the incline, back uptown. Now that we were expecting it, now that we had slept and had more energy, it did not seem as steep. Slowly and comfortably, we made our way back up, talking again as we retraced our steps and now went further. Through my mother's eyes, I saw what had changed and what remained the same since the last time she had been to the Upper East Side. She talked about where she went for concert practice as a child when she played the flute. Which subway stop she got off at, and where my grandfather occasionally dropped her off or picked her up if the weather was bad. Which of the co-ops had been around forever, and which were new. We moved at a leisurely pace.

Through that walk, more than anything else, I was conscious of how I belonged to this place. To this majestic city that lends itself to renewal and rebirth more than many other places in the world. To the promise and hope that landing somewhere new and working hard, you can build a life more closely aligned to your talent and power even if it is not valued where you come from. Whether it is true or not anymore, the feeling is still there, the electricity, a hope that cannot be quantified even though so many more elements of life can. I come from this place where, over generations and centuries, people at least tried to take their destinies into their own hands. Some did better than others, but they all did the best they could with what they had. Their descendants will always have this grit in their souls even if the stories may get lost to time.

Once we got to 69th Street, it was time to make a left, cut toward the park, and go the remaining few blocks west until we reached our destination. We had sauntered up, past row after row of venerated townhouses, taking our time up until that point, but we were getting too close to our scheduled appointment and had to pick up the pace.

Then, before we were fully mentally prepared for it, we were at the converted townhouse on 69th Street, just a block away from Central Park, with the red-and-white-striped, blue-and-yellow-starred flags outside. If we hadn't known it was a consulate, it might as well have been yet another fancy doctor's office or a discreet legal firm. The red brick façade with white-framed windows was New York understatement at its finest. We were right on time. I rang the buzzer and said we were there for our appointment. They let us in immediately since we were the only appointment for that hour due to ongoing COVID protocols. There was a vestibule with security cameras, but no metal detector, no X-ray machine, none of the full-blown security apparatus that I had experienced trying to enter US embassies or consulates abroad that may deter attacks but also make regular people feel phenomenally unwelcome and insecure. The Austrian Consulate, on the other hand, felt surprisingly accessible.

We did not have to wait for long, just a minute or two, until the diplomat who was our point of contact since we first submitted our applications came out to greet us warmly and get on with the paperwork. He was much taller than I had expected. If we were shorter than he expected, he did not let on. He was friendly and welcoming and seemed happy that we were there. He explained what we would be doing for the next hour. First we would be formally finalizing the citizenship process, and then we would apply for passports and other documents. First would be my mother, and then it would be my turn. He would help us out with everything.

My mother asked if she could show him something before we got started. Of course, he said, calm and patient, but with his eyes crinkled in a befuddled manner. It seemed like he was used to people coming in and wanting to move forward to finish their paperwork as quickly as possible. I reached into my backpack and took out the envelope of pictures that had come from the box. My mother wanted to present her grandmother, the reason why we were here in the first place, to this man, this stranger, this reverse gatekeeper. There she was, in front of the liquor store and bar that had reached such family renown, with her dog, Petey, in Vienna. There she was on the boat over. There she was, in the US, with my mother as a child. The small pieces of my great-grandmother's life that we still had accessible, from the last third of her time on this Earth, which all went in a way she could have never predicted as a girl in a small Slovakian border town.

There were few pictures, but my mother slowly shuffled through them, smiling at the memories she had and the dreams that those memories had stirred up. The tall consular officer was kind and patient, but, as a bureaucrat is wont to do, after some murmurs that showed his polite interest, he got us on with the business at hand. The official reason we were scheduled for a significant amount of his time that morning did not include looking at old pictures.

Then, suddenly, we were Austrian. First, my mother, and then I, signed the last of the paperwork in front of him to verify that we were formally Austrian. He gave us our cream-and-yellow official notification documents in formal red and white folders. It took a little while longer, but we filled out the other applications for passports, identity cards, and certificates of citizenship. At a window in the same room, they took our fingerprints for the passports and we paid the fees in exact bills, cash only. It took longer than we'd expected, a bit more than the full hour they'd allotted for us. I could understand why the consular officer wanted to move on.

As we finished, another woman came in for her appointment. She had come to Manhattan for the day from Long Island with her daughter. It made me nostalgic for the day trips "into the city," coming in on the commuter rail for lunch and a museum, that I used to take when I was sleeping over at my grandparents' house. We chatted with her a little bit as we were wrapping up. She was the "me" for her family. She was the one who put everything together, who pulled everyone along who wanted to take this journey. I guess every family who goes through a process like this needs to have a person like that, getting everything in order, keeping tabs on how things are going, making sure the flow continues. We finished up so she could take her turn to become Austrian.

When we left the consulate and emerged into the sunny late morning, it was a bit disorienting. We were Austrian now. It was done. But nothing really had changed in that hour. The New York City we were reentering was the same as the one we had left a short time before. The only thing to do, to ease that psychic dissonance, was to move, to walk, to shake out the confusion. We made a right-hand turn out of the consulate toward Central Park, which we could see clearly a block and a half away.

The plan was to get back to Penn Station for our train but to take that walk, perhaps the reverse of the one that my great-aunts and great-grandmother took to formally apply for restitution all those years ago. We had hours to go before our train back, and there was no hurry as we walked through the winding paths of southeast Central Park toward their old apartment. We were in our own movie, circumnavigating the grandstands and ambling along the relatively empty paths, seeing what we stumbled across that seemed familiar. The park was still the park, and it felt comfortingly the same. We did not talk very much, each of us lost in our own thoughts. As we shifted our angle and approached the southern end of the park, the new skinny skyscrapers that somehow sprung up into the sky like needles unnerved us. The last time we had been there, facing that direction, none of them existed.

We left the park behind in the middle of 60th Street at the Avenue of the Americas – the Americas that gave my family a new life and gave us the ability to live in peace and prosper in a way that nobody else in the family did who had experienced that war. From there, it was not far to the apartment where my mother had gone to visit her grandmother and aunts throughout her childhood. A few blocks down and around the corner from there to Carnegie Hall, past the fabled Russian Tea Room, and then after another zigzag, we were there.

The building at 161 West 54th Street, The Congress, is beautifully well-preserved. The entryway to the apartments is painted a calming gray, but the large building above looms solidly red brick. The young doorman was kind when my mother said that her grandmother and aunts used to live there, and "Would it be possible just to see the lobby?" He let us in without a second thought. My mother looked around. The lobby, she said, hadn't changed in any noticeable way. There were ornate black and white marble stone tiles, brass banisters, and an old-fashioned-looking elevator vestibule. My mother could have been going back to visit them as though 50 years had not passed.

In the lobby, these were all hallmarks of an old, fancy but not too fancy Manhattan building that no regular person can afford an apartment in anymore without rent control. My great-grandmother and great-aunts had lived there with rent control for decades. When my great-aunts left the city, in the 1970s for their sunny southern California retirement, my grandparents thought about trying to move in, to transfer the opportunity over without arousing too much suspicion. They had the same surname, after all. One Wald to another, right? Maybe nobody would even notice.

But they never seriously tried to do so. I wondered, standing there, what it would have been like to grow up visiting my grandparents within a stone's throw of Central Park rather than Coney Island. To have had the center of everything at your fingertips in a way that feels maddeningly normal instead of that quiet middle-class part of Brooklyn that was a second home to me. To have been able to go to the playground in one of the most famous parks in the world, to have that as my level of access. What kind of impressions would that have left me with? What kind of an alternate childhood would that have engendered? I would never know.

Back outside, we stopped about ten feet from the door. My mother mentioned that the rental-car area down the street used to be the parking lot where they always parked when the young doorman came running out looking for us. He had gone to get the building manager who had worked there for such a long time. Maybe he had known my great-grandmother or my great-aunts. So we went back in.

We went back in and my mother talked with the building manager for a few minutes until there was nothing more to say. The building manager had been there a long time, but not quite long enough. But since that kind of thoughtfulness and humanity is rare in midtown Manhattan, especially among strangers, we all took that extra bit of time to feel at home in a place that is in such constant churn, with such an oversized footprint of its importance in the world, that it feels like home to both everybody and nobody all at once.

You can be from there, leave, and come back; you can come from anywhere and stay. But on any given day, with any given reason to be there, you never quite know if the city will spit you back out as though you have never been there at all. Or maybe you will be lucky and you will tap into an unexpected, familiar intimacy that somehow makes it a manageable, human place. A place where anybody can work toward finding a way to belong.

PART IV
FUTURE

XVI. CONNECT

For many people, the ending would go like this: Having obtained their Austrian citizenship and passport, they set plans to move to Europe, whether Austria or elsewhere; in the 29 European nations that are part of the Schengen area, there is free movement across borders. They research options for jobs in cities that look interesting, begin interview processes, or, if they run their own business, plan to transfer it overseas.

For those not looking to work too hard or nearing retirement, southern Europe has appeal. They begin to research how far their savings and pensions can stretch and which countries will allow them to access public health systems most affordably. Imaginations may start to run wild with ideas about renovating rustic one-euro houses in quaint Italian villages or spending languid afternoons on the sunny Spanish coast. Maybe these ideas came from reading a travelogue or watching a movie. Suddenly, it all seems possible.

For me now, though, what? The journey is simply over. I have no plans to move to Europe tomorrow, next week, or anytime soon. Nothing is pushing me to those shores that seems like it would be better than the life I have built on this side of the Atlantic.

My new citizenship does feel quite permanent, and maybe that prevents my rushing into a move. I was born and grew up in the United States, and absorbed the American culture and values that surrounded me, breathing them in like air. That feels permanent. I know, in theory, with my newly acquired Austrian nationality, that nobody can take it away from me like they did my ancestors. Barring exceptional, unlikely circumstances, I am Austrian and will remain so for the rest of my life. As long as I file the necessary paperwork before they turn 14, my children – biological or adopted – will be Austrian. But it still does not feel fully real. I do not speak German or have been to the country for as long as 24 hours, but there you go. I am, technically, Austrian.

Sometimes these types of things happen serendipitously. I was paying attention at a point when people whom I did not know, whom I had never met, changed something that would deeply affect me because of what my family suffered years ago. Even if I do not know exactly what that benefit will be, I am sure there will be one. Maybe that is why I do not feel the urge to jump on the first plane and see where the wind takes me.

To close the circle, about six weeks after visiting New York, I got my new Austrian documents in the mail. The passport felt flimsy and the citizenship certificate almost looked like something I could print out myself. The identification card was very modern, though, with clear plastic cutouts and many security features. Every time I looked at it, I felt like I had found something new that was cool to see, that I hadn't noticed before. This was a high-tech identification card.

If the passport was also high-tech, I could not discern it beyond the biometric marker that now tags all passports from economically advanced countries. In a way, all new passports feel a bit fake until you start to use them, but with this one, it was jarring to see my face in that frame as an Austrian citizen. It felt like I would be playing a trick on someone if I used it. It felt like something out of a spy movie where identities shift due to necessity and convenience. I had always been identified as a US citizen. Suddenly, seeing I was Austrian so clearly on that passport, I realized that was only part of the story now and forever into the future.

With my documentation in hand, I did the last thing, the responsible thing. The thing that was my new civic duty, at least as far as my American upbringing had culturally hammered into me. I registered to vote. That was, in and of itself, a unique process. Austria is such a small country compared to the places I know best. For most, the connection and sense of place goes back generations. I suppose it is like that everywhere that most people are granted nationality. They are not like me. The act of registering showed me that mainstream Austrians were not necessarily prepared for those who would be part of their country through the process I took.

I had to register to vote through the Vienna municipal office that handles elections. The voter registration form was short and direct, but it included questions about your concrete connection to Austria. Having a passport or a citizenship certificate was not enough; they asked how close you were to the country. I went down the series of questions checking. No, I was not born in Austria. No, my parents were not born in Austria. No, I had never worked in Austria. No, I did not have a last address in Austria. And on and on it went. Until the end, the last question, when they gave you a chance since you did not fit into any of their preframed ideas about why or how someone would have a connection, to state why you should be able to vote.

My family fled the Nazi regime, I wrote in German provided by Google Translate. Before 1938, they lived in Vienna. And I included their address. I signed the form and emailed it to the proper municipal authority, with a copy of the photo page of my new passport. There were no problems, and I am now registered to vote in the district corresponding to that last address, the apartment on Klopstockgasse 29. Undertaking that first bureaucratic process with my newly issued documentation, registering to vote, finally made it feel real. I will receive a large envelope in the mail whenever there are European or Austrian elections and my vote will count.

Registering and wanting my vote to count is a distinctly American value. In many parts of the world, people are not used to democracy being so direct. They are used to political appointees and career bureaucrats being the ones who officially make things happen. Their vote does not impact the apparatus. My vote will probably not impact the Austrian apparatus, but I do not care. I am trying to navigate this new reality the best I can, applying the values and purpose I know from my upbringing. In the United States, you grow up with the idealistic notion that your vote matters. It is the way you're able to make things better.

Objectively, I can vote for things I know nothing about, are not part of my daily life, and never have been. Perhaps wanting to know your level of connection is why they have that odd questionnaire as the main part of the voter registration form. It is funny in a way. I do not have a feel for Austrian society beyond self-fulfilling stereotypes that Austrians pretend to be efficient like Germans but are slow and bureaucratic like Italians. I do not know anything about what it is like to live in Vienna now, where I will be able to vote in national elections but many who have lived there for decades cannot. It is something they seem rather upset about. I would be, too, if I were in their shoes.

Those people are disenfranchised even if they have lived in Austria for decades because Austria makes people going through the naturalization process renounce their existing citizenship without the guarantee that their Austrian citizenship will be approved. If they go through that process, they are, technically, at least for a little bit, stateless. I think that would be too risky; if I were going through that process, and, something went wrong at the tail end of it, just before I was approved as Austrian, what recourse would I have? So I can understand people not wanting to do it. And I can understand they would also resent not being able to vote to make changes in the place they have called home for years. I would wager that they also resent people like me who, to address and compensate for a historical grievance, have an alternate pathway that allows them to keep both citizenships.

The Austrians themselves – the few I got to know during this whole process – were not particularly helpful in working to encourage me, to educate me, to engage. When my mother and I finalized our official paperwork, a few pleasant form letters from government officials were included in the packet. Lovely to read, and lovely to receive positive sentiments from whoever those authorities were, but unhelpful in a practical sense. What do I do with all this now? How do people understand things? What does this place care about? What should I care about within it?

I asked for help from the few Austrians I knew at the time and was greeted with either silence or a biting comment that they'd be happy to help, but, of course, any help or guidance they'd give would be in German. The unspoken subtext was "Leave me alone, why are you asking me anyway?" So I left them alone and hoped I would meet more empathic people in the future who would come to me with as much of an open mind and heart as I was coming to them. Early on, as a newly minted Austrian, I wish there would have been a bit more understanding, a bit more kindness, to at least talk through the current political landscape, give me a crash course in culture beyond schnitzel and skiing, so I could start with some firm ground to stand on.

But this response was indicative of their ambivalence, discomfort, and understanding, or lack thereof, with their families' roles in the horror that my family ended up on the wrong side of. It had little to do with me. It was good to be exposed to it from the outset. It made me realize that my openness could be greeted with hostility or suspicion. It is one thing to understand that my citizenship would right a historical wrong. It is another to look directly into the face of someone who has successfully navigated that abstract process, knowing they now have the same rights as you, and not knowing what they think about their new country or what they plan to do with those rights.

Without speaking German well, without having someone available at the outset who seemed like they could help me understand more about the culture, knowing that it would be years until I felt like myself in the language even if I could speak it better, I tried to find ways to learn, to relate to what it might be like there now. I tried to find ways to connect from across the ocean. With limited resources and not knowing where to start, I did a deep dive into one of the few relatively recent Austrian shows on Netflix.

Much of what I first learned about modern Austrian culture came from a black-comedy soap opera so dark and bleak that sometimes it was hard to tell if the joke had gone too far or if that is just how Austrians are – taking things to the extreme. Pick one of the following topics: antisemitism, corruption, gold-digging, incest, manipulation, reparations. The topics, the themes, not shying away from taboo or personal and moral hypocrisy were all there, taken to surreal conclusions. I laughed a lot. I cringed a lot. I felt like I got something out of it – a black mirror into a world I was now linked to, warts and all.

On some level, it is a joke to say I understand something about a specific culture and society through a television show, but what else can I say? It is a joke that should not be funny, yet it is. It is like people in the '80s saying they knew the United States from watching Miami Vice. Except I do not think most of those people were able to vote in the United States. But without going to Austria and experiencing it, this is what I had to start with for now.

When our first Austrian elections rolled around, which happened to be the presidential elections in the fall of 2022, I had to do my own research. I had to understand this new system while figuring out what was going on over there and what issues I most cared about in this new context. I had to understand the candidates and what they represented. See whose platforms resonated with me. Long before we received large envelopes in the mail, I was doing my homework, taking my new civic responsibilities seriously even if I had to use plug-ins to translate websites into English. Once the ballots arrived, I used a cellphone app to instantaneously translate what they said and the voting instructions into a language I could understand.

These elections were structured so that if nobody won an outright majority, a run-off election would be held between the top two candidates. The process gave me a bit of measured peace to vote for who I wanted without having to make a risk-based calculation of whether I thought my vote would push someone I was ideologically opposed to into office. So at the same dining-room table in my parents' house where so many parts of this Austrian journey had taken place, I voted for the candidate who I thought best represented what a future could be. You wouldn't believe what party my candidate was from, however: the Beer Party.

I am still not clear whether the party is a joke or a publicity stunt by its fearless leader, who is also the lead singer of a punk band. Either way, it is certainly a punk-rock thing to do to offer hope against the fear that the right wing might be tiptoeing its way toward fascism, showing there are creative ways to maneuver even if they seem overwhelming or oppressive. It is clearly a punk-rock thing to question the status quo and ask the types of questions that make other people uncomfortable. It is absolutely a punk-rock thing to demand an alternative and, if you do not see one, become it yourself.

I was surprisingly happy and proud to be able to vote for that candidate. After the elections were over, quite a few others also seemed to have made the same choice, particularly those who lived where I might if I were to try to move to Vienna. It gave me a lot more hope than I initially had. Maybe there would be a way I could fit into this seemingly strait-laced society even if I was not sure exactly what that might be. Maybe it would be fine to take my time, dig a little bit deeper, and see where it all might go.

XVII. RELATE

I would like to go and spend some time in Austria, of course. I want to experience a real sense of place to understand if all I feel is ghosts or if there is hope for a new and dynamic future of which I can be a part. Relying on a television comedy to get a sense of a place and its culture is silly, even if I did so because it was the least bad option. I still do not know if there is something there that I can relate to, that would truly feel like another home, albeit halfway around the world.

Now that I can stay without impediments, I would like to see if I feel I belong there. Spend a few days, a few weeks, a few months in all these different places that are not far apart. Breathe the air, eat the food, feel the ground under my feet. See if the sum of all the parts feels like a type of home that I did not know I had, that I did not know would be available, even if I now know that my ancestors lived there for hundreds of years and probably never thought they would have to leave – until they did.

Austria, and Vienna in particular, have such a strange history within Europe, itself a continent of strange coincidences and happenstances intermingled with destruction. There is that sense of grandeur left over in Vienna, which has only recently recovered its status as the second-largest German-speaking city in the world. From an outsider's perspective who has now read a lot as a hobbyist on the topic, it seems like it isn't clear yet for Vienna how to move forward. The city is gaining new renown as both a wonderful place to live in terms of infrastructure and amenities and an awful place because of how Austrians relate to the foreigners who continue to make up a sizable minority of the Viennese population. I feel like some of what forced my family out, the positive changes that many people found too radical at the time, like affordable public housing, are gaining a new life on their own and people are recognizing they were ahead of their time.

Vienna's quality public housing system consistently pushes it to the apex of global "livable cities" ratings despite the city being extremely expensive in other ways and the country having one of the largest wealth gaps in Europe. Most people in Vienna take its beautiful, subsidized housing for granted as an integral part of how things are done and always have been. However, public housing was never a guaranteed success, nor did people likely envision it would still be touted a hundred years later. It was one of the main public benefit projects in socialist Red Vienna during the interwar period. At the time, it was widely considered an expensive flight of fancy pushed forward by all those Jews who were not real Austrians, did not share Austrian values, and had to prove again and again and again that they were worthy. And now it is something that other countries want to learn how to do better, in which Austrians take great pride.

Being ahead of your time, like those who championed the public housing system, is often an isolating and unsettling experience. There are doubts, and questions if you are seeing things with clear eyes and why others do not seem to want to move things in a way you find obvious. Now, seeing how the rest of the world looks on in awe, I hope somewhere that those who championed this project and others – benefiting people regardless of where they came from or their economic circumstances – are smiling.

I would like to go to Vienna, of course, but in a way that feels like I'm seeing its everyday fabric, not just visiting the downtown of majestic buildings and long-frozen glory. To somewhere around Klopstockgasse 29 in Hernals, which now seems to be a lovely and low-key district, and to the hiking trails in the famed Viennese woods. From Hernals, you can easily get to both the woods and the city center on public transportation and give yourself peace among the trees or extravagance at fancy restaurants and theaters, whatever strikes your fancy. That, to me, would be ideal. When the city is overwhelming, the woods would still be there, but you would have the best of the city a stone's throw away. If my family were still there, living in that property, I wonder how much it would be worth. How many other people see value in living with that type of access in today's world?

But I do not want to stop with that last known address in Hernals. I would like to go to all the places I found as part of this process and see what they are like. I want to make a loop starting and ending in Vienna while recognizing that it is not the only part of my story and that an Austrian identity card does not only give me access to Vienna. Within the European Union, the reconstituted borderless Schengen zone goes well beyond the reaches of the Austro-Hungarian Empire. It will let me go to Czechia, Slovakia, and Poland. It will let me take that all-American of things, a road trip, to the places my people came from and were once within the same empire. My family left when that all crumbled, but it is back in its own way. The European Union and the fall of communism have taken those 80 years of chaos of splintering places that had been inexorably linked for centuries and stitched them back together much more broadly, hopefully with stronger thread.

From Vienna, I would rent a car and go to the eastern end of the Czech Republic, to Přívoz, the suburb of Ostrava, that first important stop where my grandfather was born and Hans Fischer was sent to his death. I would like to see the nearby Freud family home in Moravia, too, to think that somehow I am connected, in a subconsciously universal way, to that most famous, most emblematic of Austrian Jews. The Freuds, too, were only Austrian for one generation, as they would be considered now. Like my family was. And like I am again.

From there, I would cross the border, but of my own accord, as my own choice, and go to Poland. Part of my father's side of the family was from Galicia. The region had the most backwoods group of Jews in the Austro-Hungarian Empire, and I am curious what those endless stretches of farmland, not unlike the American Midwest in spirit, feel like today. In my research, I found a Yizkor (funerary) book, one of many that exist to commemorate the more rural Jewish communities that were completely razed during the war. It had the names of the extended Hand family members who were not able to get out in time either, summarily murdered. The town they were from translates from Polish as "Wasteland," which does not bode well standing on its own. But if we ran away from all the things that did not seem pleasant, we would not be able to appreciate beauty when it is there. It is a stop on the journey I will need to make, whether I want to or not. It is a stop that might send me running, but I will need to feel that for myself, to understand why they, too, ran as soon as possible.

From there, I would go due south, to the four or five towns in Slovakia that I have flagged. The places where my great-grandparents were born, where they married, where the Waldapfels can be traced back nearly three centuries, just across the border from what used to be the Ottoman Empire. Waldapfels can be traced back to the mid-1700s using the tools we have now, but my best guess is they lived there much longer. Jews within the Austro-Hungarian Empire were required to take on Germanic surnames in 1798; before then, they followed the traditional patrilineal naming traditions that still exist religiously today. This was the first time Jews within the Dual Monarchy were forced to take on public identities that would allow them to be characterized in the same way as other mainstream ethnic groups. Someone who took on one of those surnames in the late 1700s could easily have been born in the mid-1700s, but before that, the trail goes cold because there really is no way to trace it. The names did not remain the same.

I feel deep within my bones, in a way that is hard to explain, that they were part of that place much longer than the records can show. Going back who knows how many generations, maybe a thousand years? I would find a lodge or cabin to stay in and spend some time in that part of the Carpathian Mountains that crests along northern Slovakia, forming a natural border with southern Poland. I would take the time to explore the woods, go up and down hills and mountains, see the sights from the solitude of the crests, and feel the peace of the populated valleys. I would feel if my love of the woods and hiking, that form of contentment and peace, goes beyond my memories of a bucolic early childhood in the Hudson Highlands of New York State, my explorations of craggy islands on foot in Ireland, or my attempts to wear myself out at higher altitudes in central Mexico. If it comes from a deeper, elemental place, where this type of environment, no matter where it is in the world, feels like home. Because it was home to so many for so long.

And from there, it would be easy enough to close the loop, driving back down the highway into Vienna from Bratislava. An imperial loop to trace what I can find, feel whatever it is I end up feeling, from my Austro-Hungarian roots, where I can now re-root if I choose. Even if no survivors live anywhere near any of these places. Even if the people who look like me no longer live there. Even if they were all pushed out and forgotten, barring the occasional memorial here or there, which may or may not be in a central location, may or may not be designed to force acknowledgment or remembrance on all who pass by and notice. Many of these places, as far as I can tell, are still unwilling to grapple with the fact that they expelled their own, pushed them out so easily, so recently, to fates uncertain but with odds certainly not in their favor.

It is a strange feeling to know that my family was only officially from one specific place for one generation and to know I have access to this broader plane of origin as a result. I would not be so directly eligible for any of these other nationalities at this point, even if they all descend from the same empire, the same past, the same history. This last stop on the journey, as awful as it was by the end, is what enables this loop to be closed now and allows me to get on the road. It is amazing to think I can do this, that the only thing in the way is finding the time and making it happen. Now I am the only one in the way.

XVIII. SHIFT

When I consider this process as a whole, it has required me to adjust many preconceived notions. About myself and my place in the world. About where I can find a center of belonging. About the people who came before me and their relationships with these precarious notions and ideas of what determines a self that frame who we are and where we're going.

In my conversations with others who unearthed their family history, the impression is inevitably, at least initially, one of resolute determination. Determination to validate the inhumane experiences that their family members suffered and survived, even if nearly a century has passed. Determination to see the process through despite the curious machinations of bureaucracy in what is usually a foreign language. Determination that seeks to rise above the trauma that people suffered, since they are gone and it can no longer be addressed, not in any direct way but at least acknowledged using today's more nuanced understanding. Determination to elevate themselves and where they are at and, for most, more importantly, give the benefits of these connections to their children. It is part of all our history, and we are just the vessels through which having this type of recognition gives it a different type of meaning.

These are not just personal histories, even if that is the lens that people undertaking these processes most commonly use. They are part of world history, and there is certainly meaning in my undertaking this process to understand those on the other side of the victimization of my ancestors. The people in mainstream Austrian society, whose representatives allowed this to take place. And the people in mainstream Austrian society today, who have now opened the door to reconciliation for what happened almost a century ago. Now that it is done, I seek out Austrians in my international environs and tell them that I, too, am Austrian, although my German is nonexistent. They all speak fluent English, so the conversations flow more easily than they would if I tried to approximate the words in my very, very, very, bad German. "Really?" they inevitably ask. "Is it a family connection?"

"Sort of," I say. "I am not sure if you were paying attention, who knows what sticks with people in the news these days anyway. A few years ago, the citizenship law was changed, to let people whose ancestors were victims of the fascist regimes apply for restoration citizenship, and we qualified ..." at which point, some people do remember and it clicks. They usually are quiet at first, waiting for me to volunteer information, not knowing that I am happy to be open about the process and have no real interest in what their ancestors were doing before, during, and after the war. I do not know if they are thinking of their own family stories on the other side of that invisible fence, of who was a victim and who was a perpetrator, but they are gracious and kind. They've never met someone who had gone through with the process before, who was open about it and told them. They ask questions. They want to know more.

It brings me joy to be accepted like this, with nobody questioning whether I am a "real" Austrian, even without having the language. Rather, they seem to acknowledge the forced interruption in my family's journey. Some are excited to learn that my family story coalesced in New York City. They have been there, too. It is a wonderful place. They ask if I have been to Vienna, what I think about the city beyond the castle walls, the outer rings where normal people live. They are intrigued and surprised to hear that my family is from Hernals, which was rough back then but where many professionals live now because the rent is more affordable. I tell them I have been to Vienna, but only for a short time, and would love to go back for a few months to really get a feel for the city knowing that I can live there if I want to.

There is a new sort of rapport that feels natural in these exchanges. I am happy I can be open about what happened without personal anger. I am relieved and excited that they can respond similarly and it feels like we are on a level field, discussing normal things about a place where I can also belong. I can make new friends and forge new connections, and I do not have to worry about strange old feelings that might be sloshed up in the process.

Where I have noticed ambivalence, though, is among those of us who have undertaken the journey. There is so much questioning about what it means personally. For many, just like for me, it does not change much, at least not in the short term. It offers more options, with fewer bureaucratic hurdles, but it does not change the daily reality in a world still far removed from whatever those possibilities might be. It seems most of these people whose ancestors fled, at least the ones I am exposed to, are doing well for themselves. As am I. I have a feeling that many would have been able to move between countries and make major life changes even before this option was available, before it became so easy to do. Just as I did for myself.

Although it might not change much in the short term, successfully restoring birthright citizenship that was denied for generations gives access to this new community of restless transplants – as one person I spoke with called it, the Viennese Jewish Diaspora. Our ancestors, the ones who made it through, went wherever they could survive. Many of them thrived wherever they ended up, having developed the tools of adaptability as a part of the Vienna that is still elevated as a shining beacon of modern history during its golden age, before they had to flee. It gives a new base of commonalities, a new community for those who might be looking for it. I have certainly found it so.

Conversations with those in this community quickly open into deep revelations. The type of immediate intimacies I have not had since being a college student are formed. It is a beautiful thing in a world where we are pressured to hide that level of openness, lest we seem too intense, too vulnerable, too something.

We recognize that going through the process blasts open a world of mobility – be it temporary or permanent – that becomes more and more restrictive by the year, with precision biometry replacing the relatively forgiving chaos of personal judgment to filter people at these international borders. Everything in order, *Alles in Ordnung*, takes on another meaning when that order can be made permanently active or inactive with a couple of keystrokes on a computer, with little or no recourse for an individual who might need that bit of saving grace.

As Europe closes off behind a digital wall, as the United States has, I wonder what the full repercussions will be. For people like my family, both the first Austrians who came and opened it up for everyone else, and those on the other side of my family who would certainly not be allowed in or out now.

I have been focused on the Austrians in my family for the obvious reason that their experiences are the ones that have forged this story into being. The Polish corner of my family, on my father's side, in contrast, was a whole different reality from the Austrians, as I also found out during this process. When I think about that Polish group, who were out on the far-flung reaches of the Austro-Hungarian empire, and then folded into the rolling farmland of southern Poland, I know that today's harsh digitization of identity, of unrelenting border control, would not ever have given them a chance to leave Europe and start life anew.

While we do not know why my great-grandfather left Poland under an assumed name, he did. And once he entered the United States, he went back to using his old name. Doing so was not illegal at the time, and it is fully documented on his naturalization paperwork from a decade after his arrival. It would never be allowed to happen today in an age where full background checks would preclude immigration success.

We can guess that my great-grandfather, born Isador (spelled many ways on different documents) Hand (always spelled the same) but using the name Isaac Katz for a while, deserted the Austro-Hungarian army during World War I. And we can guess at the family's interest in him getting out once Poland became independent if people who knew and disapproved of his actions came into positions of authority. That is what makes sense, putting the story together from afar, although we have no proof. He disappeared, as far as the Polish authorities were concerned, and I am sure that was fine for them. It was also fine for him since he lived out the rest of his life as a butcher in Manhattan, where he made ends meet and his US-born son – my other grandfather – catapulted up the social mobility stratosphere.

But nobody can disappear like that anymore and rebuild a life from nothing, with whatever name and identity you choose, just because your old life did not work for you anymore. The next best thing is the ability to just be able to go, to make that trip without anyone questioning what will happen at the border, under your own name, so that you, too, can start anew.

XIX. BUILD

I am convinced that most people want to feel they are working toward something positive in their lives – whether that takes the form of work, family, personal accomplishments, or any other driving force. Depending on the cultures that people come from, the things that are elevated in their lives, and their own personalities, this drive takes on a life of its own as they navigate toward a fruitful life. They have worked hard for their success and are proud.

Most of the time, this path assumes stability. Most people aren't as peripatetic as I am, and if they are, it is almost certainly not by choice. Most are content to continue to build on a legacy, in the same place, with the same rhythms and patterns that offer belonging and comfort, assuming the status quo will continue quietly floating on its way, taking them seamlessly out with the tide.

As I have seen with my family's story, stability and comfort are a luxury and might be the exception rather than the rule. It cannot be assumed, especially as things change around us and we, as small pieces of the puzzle, have little or no control over how these changes play out in the world. When we are lucky, we have the resources to counter the waves and find another place that will allow us to continue our lives in relative peace and prosperity. When we are privileged, we can surf on the crest and find a way to make it tolerable even if there is much we disagree with. When we are neither lucky nor privileged, we are subjected to the whims of others who value their own well-being over anything else. If we try to go somewhere else under these circumstances, the most common way is via euphemistically mentioned alternative channels.

Is it possible in our modern age to have any control over these bigger winds, chaotically blowing to and fro? I do not think so. Professionally, I have worked in the international policy space for many years. When I started working with bigger names, like the government agencies and the international organizations you read about in the news, I realized they might seem to set agendas and priorities, but even they are responding and reacting to events. The long arms of government that seem to have outsized resources to dictate programs and policy fret about the body politic. They worry about maintaining their budgets and supporting the priorities of those who set those budgets. The same is true for international organizations, working hard to keep all their member-states engaged and happy, unwilling to stick their necks out over problematic trends until they become the new normal and the funding countries demand action.

People learn, often the hard way, that they must build and rebuild no matter where they are in this world, no matter where they end up, even if it is a nowhere land they never would have expected themselves to end up in indefinitely. Whenever I have gotten to know people who have personally experienced and understand the fluidity of these kinds of situations, regardless of whether they are migrants themselves, there is a complicated undercurrent. It is hard to describe in ways that do not challenge the idea that society is stable and that our lives will pass in a predictable trajectory within that stability, exceptional in their ordinariness. Nobody ever initially thinks they will be the ones who must flee. Nobody thinks these types of stories, which happen in places so far away, in times so remote, will happen to them. They are initially thought of as panicked stories of paranoia from people who imagine the worst and do not know how to hope for the best.

Until they do happen and people are forced out of their lives because of war, because of crime, because of violence, because of poverty, regardless of whether all their documents are in order. When things are that bad, people take whatever route is available to them, legality (in whatever way different people understand the nuances of that word for migration purposes) be damned. That is the modern human condition to me – self-preservation, with a belief in one's ability to work hard and a dash of hope that the worst won't happen to them. That they'll be the ones who make it, and these stories about dying of dehydration in the desert, being pushed off a boat because they cannot pay the smugglers, or smothering in cargo bays will not happen to them. They will be able to make it to the other side and be fine. They will be more than fine. They will survive and they will thrive.

In story after story after story reported from these shifting zones subject to migratory attempts, from Mediterranean dinghies to trekking through the Darién Gap between North and South America, to landing on isolated Australian islands and everywhere in between, everyone hopes for the best despite the risks and, in some cases, clear evidence that it doesn't work out for most of them. None of us can bear the thought of our lives ending in such ignominious ways, our stories cut short because we push for something better, something we consider noble but is seen as less than that or even criminal by others.

The worst does happen. Anyone paying attention sees those flashes of tragedy, and, if they're inclined to dig deeper, they read the stories of those who died just trying to get ahead, trying to make things better for themselves, their parents, and their children. In the same way that we all would, in the same way that my family did about a century ago, in the same way that almost everyone can understand – especially those in the United States – if they dug just a little deeper into how their family got to where they are now. It is not that hard to find the relics, the records if they want to.

The question is, do people want to? Especially those who, at least for now, are on the right side, the lucky side, of the equation. When you see old photos in a museum exhibition or sort through the banker's box that most families have with disorganized old photographs, it is jarring and unsettling to realize how easily our direct ancestors, with faces that look uncannily similar, could have been you in another place or time. If someone can sit with that discomfort, if they can try to imagine the desperation, the frustration, the barriers and walls being erected where once there was openness and opportunity, I think the reason for these decisions to build barriers being made would be different, and so would the decisions themselves. If someone can take the time to really understand a story that directly relates to them and be clear and honest about whether that grandparent, uncle, or cousin would have had the same opportunity for movement and reinvention now, I think there would be a different kind of reality.

"Times were different then" is something I have heard from people who do not care to do this type of deep dive, who do not care to put themselves in the shoes of their ancestors. What I want to say to these people is in what way exactly were times different? In what way exactly did people have different hopes and dreams, different levels of persecution and deprivation? Please help me understand these differences because, frankly, I do not see them. Or if there were any real differences then, it was probably that people were worse off. That poverty was wider spread, opportunities were more limited for people who did not already have them, and communication was less consistent and slower. That made people incredibly willing to stick it out wherever they could go.

If people sat down and understood their own family stories better, with clear eyes and open hearts, I do not think they would be able to say with a straight face that times were so different that obstacles should be erected to prevent people who could contribute from moving freely. Times were different in some ways, but I think it was more about structure than our human wants, needs, and desires. European empires were banging up against each other like tectonic plates, and globally they were still causing mass subjugation of broad swaths of the planet. World War II forced a new type of world order, and the Europe of today, which Austria is now a constitutionally neutral part of, was unfathomable. This is the piece I keep close to my heart when thinking about my grandfather and what he would have thought about the world today. About the person I am and the way I see the world. I wonder if the Austria he grew up in, the Austria he rejected wholesale as soon as he could make that choice for himself, would be one he would recognize today and feel worthy of our reconsideration and reconnection.

I will have to go back and see for myself, but everything I have personally experienced makes me hopeful. My family left to build a better life during what is probably the worst period in modern European history to be living in Central Europe, and without doubt, the worst period to be a Jew there. They were lucky to be able to trickle out when they did. They could not have anticipated how bad it would get for the loved ones they left behind.

But they also could not have anticipated what would come after – building up a solid body politic that respects as many differences as is reasonably possible in a continent that was at war with itself for the better part of recorded history. In this sense, I find the European Union to be an incredibly idealistic and romantic entity. When I flipped through the pages of European passports and saw things written in nearly 30 languages, I was floored. The American passport has four pages at the beginning, in English, reminding you that when you travel, you must abide by the rules of wherever else in the world you are, which may be different from those in the United States. Is this really something people need to be reminded of?

These pages showing the same sentence in 20-plus languages, ensuring that people throughout Europe can commonly understand, is what it physically looks like when you recognize the various types of entities that make up the whole. Each with its past, present, and future, interconnected in its issues but willing to work toward making those differences a strength for the greater good and try to limit a spiral of destruction it knows all too well and experienced directly.

This type of rebirth gives me hope that not only rises but envelops our bodies and blankets us in a sense that destruction does not have to be pointless. People can learn. People can try not to make the same mistakes and, as a global village, can start to move on and build something better than what came before.

XX. BE

Even though this process has been difficult, forcing me to acknowledge family grief and trauma that I am sure more than a few would prefer to have let fade away to the vagaries of time and memory, it has been worth it. At first, practically, I thought it would be worth it for that extra flexibility that I might get even if I could not, and still cannot, define whether I need it. I don't know whether this lifelong unsettled feeling will end up settling down or if having the option to up and go will be necessary. As I have aged and found stability in my life, I had thought the restlessness might fall by the wayside, consigned to a version of myself that is content to live in the past, captured in images and words but gone from the day-to-day.

Instead, the time and patience it has taken me to understand a complicated and traumatic past has become more about a feeling that I was previously unable to put into words. It has allowed me to wrap my head around identity not being unitary or binary even if others only see small facets of the multitudes we all contain. There are oh-so-many different, more creative ways to consider these pieces of being or belonging. And knowing where you come from, in all the complexity of that phrase, makes it so much easier. With that knowledge and understanding has come so much more.

I still do not have a succinct phrase or quippy shorthand that says exactly what this feeling is. I am proud of where I come from in the broadest sense of that sometimes polemic expression. I am proud of what my ancestors were able to do, how they created worlds for themselves no matter where they were, how I was born into the American tapestry because of that. I am saddened to know beyond a doubt that so much was left to be forgotten of those worlds once they were razed. I am happy with what I have been able to do so far and the openness and curiosity I bring in my short time on this wonderful and complicated Earth.

This journey has been so much more than that. I have pushed the boundaries of what I understood as a child, revisiting them as an adult. I have been able to relate to the past in a more relevant way than ever before. This genesis, coming back around to complete the circle and starting anew, releases me from thinking that I need to be a certain way. I can comfortably embrace the complexities of who I am since that is what my ancestors had to do, too. It opens me up, liberates me, to how our past and present mingle, flow, and pulse to create a future that can be as open as we want it to be if we are brave enough to imagine it, if we are unafraid of centering that elusively genuine sense of self, if we don't try to escape who we are because we believe it will be too much.

It has allowed me to see my ancestors as people, the same as those alive today. They had their own versions of openness and complexity, with things said and unsaid. Even though I cannot commune with them and ask why they did what they did, I have grown to understand them more. I can make my best guesses and inferences based on how I know my family is: quiet and private. I can try to understand and empathize with what I know did happen. I can find the historical understanding, both the personal documentation and the broader waves, ebbing and flowing into what later makes it into the history books, the official narrative of those times, eventually becoming the shortcut of a common cultural understanding. I can unite those two, the micro and the macro, one family's story and journey and how it relates to the big picture they experienced but could not control. They could only process, react, and do their best with the resources available. Especially being what they were, somewhere toward the middle to bottom of their adopted Austrian society. Which I am sure they also knew, even if they would not have wanted to talk about it in those words.

When we are small, these people are elevated, exalted, larger than life. They can do no wrong because they are the ones with the power whom you know about, who are showing you the world in a way that, by definition, will always seem normal. After all, that is how things are presented when you do not know any other way. As children, we do not question these realities. Or if we do, our questions are often dismissed as flights of creative fancy by those whose version of reality takes precedence. As adults, we start to see the cracks and can learn how to push, pull, and weave them together and make meaning for ourselves. This is, at the least, what I have tried and am still trying to do.

Most importantly, the difference compared to when I started this process is that I have a son. He is a baby, in awe and wonder of a world that has been nothing but loving and kind to him, with no scarcity or hate. We are fortunate to have a stable place to live and healthy food for us and him. He is warm when it is cold. When he cries, we can feed him, change his diaper, and calm him down. He is a happy baby, smiling at the neighbors, especially when they greet him as he goes out in his stroller.

All the clichés people say about having a child are true. The world changes and expands. Things look and feel different. When he was born, I wondered how we all start so small and helpless and turn into the strange and dangerous creatures we eventually become as adults. After only a few months, he is laughing and playing, blissfully unaware of the complexity he was born into.

When he grows older, he will do what we all do. He will question his parents and let us know unequivocally that we did everything wrong. He will go out with his friends and do things that are reckless but fun, things that most people stop doing as they calm down and realize that the adventures they laughed about in their early 20s really could have been dangerous. He will reckon with his own identity and become whoever he ultimately becomes. Whatever the outcome, whoever he becomes, I will do my best to help him understand that this is his history and he should not take it lightly.

His life will bring him his own challenges, but I hope they are nothing like his ancestors endured. I imagine him on a gap year enjoying the ability to work in Europe at the same age my grandfather – his namesake – left Europe behind to look for work wherever they would have him. The ability to be an integral part of so many different places, with so few restrictions, that my son will enjoy as his birthright was not born of ease. It comes from his ancestors choosing to protect themselves as best they could from a racist and hateful war by leaving their homes. He needs to know that, even if it is a more complicated story than most children need to understand. From my own experience, I know it is the only way he will be at ease with himself and those who came before him.

After becoming this other person on paper – Austrian and European – I can now move forward as an integrated whole of a person in a way I could not before. I can recognize and acknowledge my upbringing in all its communicated and uncommunicated complexity, all its unspoken fortune and misfortune. It allows me to know, beyond a doubt, that in many ways we were lucky. I am lucky. I can say, reasonably certain, that most others suffering through racism and ethnic atrocities are not so lucky today.

I can ask: What can I do to move through this world better, more congruently? I can embody those hopes and dreams even as they may take shape in a way wholly unimaginable to others back then. I can continue to learn, deepen my understanding of these realities, and connect with people so they can ask these questions and try to live out our brief time on the planet in a way that gets us to the essence of our being while trying to leave things a little better than we inherited them. I can teach my son that this is the legacy that he must in some way uphold.

All of this together brings me tremendous joy and excitement. Joy is an elusive notion that is becoming harder and harder to find as we live in a world that is both more connected but also more mechanized, a world that is less spontaneous, less organic, less natural. For me, joy is what can come out of these unpredictable coincidences and flights of fancy when we let the unexpected beauty and excitement of being human wash over us. Joy is when we leave ourselves open to possibilities and see they are open to us, experiencing what they might be in a different way. It is what might make us think, feel, and be more than we know we already are.

If we lead with true openness and curiosity, our lives are bigger and better as a result. They expand geometrically as we grow, learn, and share, and hopefully we can do the same to the lives of others. I am not naïve, and I know this is easier said than done. We can all start somewhere, though, to plant the seeds to make this world a better place and share our joy with the world as a natural part of being.

To me, joy is about discovery and belonging. Joy is about feeling we are in the right place, at the right time, as the right person, letting our internal light shine the brightest it can. This feeling changes as we do, as we grow and move in the world. A favorite toy at age five is not usually the same one by ten. The excitement of the possibilities of a night out at age 25 is well-tempered 15 years later. What brought us joy a few years ago may not bring us the same amount now. It oscillates depending on where we are, what we need. But the thoughtless routine, the monotony, the patterns we find ourselves falling into without quite realizing it also closes us off from those possibilities. It closes us off from how we can experience people and places, different things that will bring us to a state of joy and becomes more elusive. Even having clear knowledge of what will bring us into that joyful state becomes harder to find. The more routine our lives are, the more closed off they feel, and the more enclosed we become.

Feeling that joy can bring us to that elusive flow state where everything feels perfect and you would not change a thing as you roll in the waves and undulations of the here and now. There is no second-guessing, no questioning what may or may not be. Joy lets us know that we continue to grow, moving through this world and experiencing the things that make us feel alive, to see and feel things in a beautiful, new way because we have come to a new and different understanding about what we experience. What we take from that, in turn, also changes. So do the things that do not serve us, that we must leave behind.

I leave behind the idea that I need to belong to only one place, in only one static, uncompromising, heavy point in time. I can see things differently. I can be comfortable and open with the multitudes that I have always contained but have flicked away in trying to conform, for reasons I do not always feel I need to explain anymore. I can be this integrated person I never could before. I can feel those pieces sit with each other, in comfort, not tension, even if I still do not understand what they all fully mean. I can give my son a head start and hopefully give him answers to questions I never thought to ask. He can be his own person more easily and integrate his own version of what happened, what before him was passed down through feelings rather than words, and what he wants to be.

Maybe because this meaning-making has happened as an adult, I will never fully understand it or move through it naturally. Maybe I just need to accept it and move on, through the doors that open, wherever they may lead. Maybe that was what my grandfather did when he went with his gut and left because he had to, because he saw no other option in 1926 Vienna and built his life elsewhere, trusting it would all work out because there was no alternative.

I have always had options, maybe too many, and maybe I have looked for them to avoid having to wrestle with such a complicated, personal, intergenerational past I never knew about, never associated with, never wanted to know about, never knew I would want to know about. I had always thrown myself at those options openly, those that seemed more important than the regular worlds I inhabited. It has been wonderful and liberating, but now I know I could never truly ignore a past that was always there and turn it into something that never existed.

It was, like that banker box underneath my parents' teak credenza, always waiting to be opened, at the right time, for the right reasons. And now I have done the hard work of digging, focused and purposeful, turning over the topsoil to see what lies underneath, to plant a new garden. To root. To belong.

I can live the joy of who I am and where I come from, hard as it may have been at times, much as my family might have wanted to shield me from knowing this reality, thinking it was for my own good without ever knowing whom I would become or what I would be capable of. Without knowing that, in fact, I did need to know what happened. I needed to know what happened both for myself and the life I did not know was yet to come.

I have done that already and found what I could find. The rest is lost for now.

I am not lost. I am out of the labyrinthine confusion in my head and can see the path forward more clearly. I am beginning to find my way.

ACKNOWLEDGMENTS

This book has been a labor of love over many years. What began as a way to simply process the strange and emotional experience that I had somehow stumbled into when applying for Austrian citizenship through an unexpected process seemed like it could be organized a bit better and potentially take on a life of its own. I tried my best to capture what happened during the process and my complex feelings about it in a way that would resonate with people who do not necessarily have this exact story and can relate to it more universally. Although the story is from a uniquely Jewish experience, I firmly believe that many of these experiences apply to anyone whose family fled trauma and then tried to move on to avoid burdening future generations.

This is not a typical memoir or standard book about uncovering a family's history. It was never meant to be. There are many such books, particularly about someone uncovering family involvement in World War II decades afterward, whether on the side of the victims or perpetrators. This book was meant to explore what it feels like to re-create a family story while explaining the practical implications for our world. This world today that we live in and, for the most part, cannot opt out of, is increasingly digitally connected but physically impenetrable for many who happen to be born in places that do not offer opportunities for their citizens to grow. When considering my own family's history, if they had been of today's world and in a place where similar events were happening, I doubt I would be around and able to tell this story 80-something years later.

That realization has pushed me to memorialize this experience of both uncovering a past that seemed to have been put aside and having the agency and good fortune to reclaim ownership of an identity that was left behind in name but not in the essence and soul of what one of their descendants became. I hope the musings that drive this circuitous storyline are interesting and engaging. I hope they allow people to consider their own relationship with their globalized past and present, thinking ahead to the potential of the future, and the strange ways that the past has a way of sneaking back around until you can no longer ignore it.

I am grateful for my editors and readers who are willing to grapple with the complexity of these nuanced situations, considering their own place in this strange world we all inhabit. I look forward to hearing thoughts from readers. Once this book is out in the world, any intention I may have around the message or text will be irrelevant and people will take from it whatever reflects back on them and their lives.

In my research to prepare the evidence for the Austrian authorities, two dear friends provided invaluable help. Mark Gilbert unfailingly found answers to specific questions I had about my family lineage, with limited information and no fluent German, Czech, Slovak, or Yiddish language skills. Lukas Keller, with his parents Ullrich and Maria Keller, patiently reviewed and interpreted family letters that opened the door to what my family experienced during 1937–1938 in their own words. They both made me feel like becoming European in today's world would be a worthwhile endeavor and have supported and cheered me on every step of the way. I am so grateful for their encouragement.

Getting this book out into the world, ready to take on a life of its own, would not have been possible without so much help and support from kind friends and colleagues. Ellen Cooper did the initial hard work of helping me give form to somewhat unstructured ramblings that needed to be shaped into something more digestible. She helped me figure out how to present the best version of this work from the beginning of the process and I am deeply appreciative. My beta readers gave me the confidence to push forward – thanks to Elly Berke, Kit Cangardel, Beth Callaghan, Erin Creley, Alexis Ditkowsky, Lily Ehelbracht, Tracy Lieberman, Louise Vigeant, and Mary Claire Whitaker. Lai-Yee Yau, thank you for your multiple readings and helping me get to a finish line that sometimes seemed like it kept receding. Deep gratitude to Fedor van Rijn, who reviewed and copy-edited the first full version of the manuscript. All of you, and so many more, cheered me all along the way.

Reflection on this memoir-writing process was the basis of an academic journal article I wrote. The article was published in a special edition of *Ethical Space* focused on third-generation Holocaust storytelling in late 2023. The article forced me to consider much of this narrative from a more analytic perspective. I do not pretend to be a specialist in communications or storytelling and can only speak as a person who is, in general, very self-aware. I deeply appreciated the opportunity to frame this process from another perspective. David Beard was very helpful in terms of framing the content for that article, and Tess Scholfield-Peters was a magnificent editor. Thanks to both.

Government institutions can sometimes seem impenetrable, but I have worked with kind professionals throughout. Suzy Snyder, then at the US Holocaust Memorial Museum, was nothing but helpful and encouraging when I reached out to the museum in 2021. I appreciate the time that Moritz Wein, at the Austrian Federal Ministry of Education, Science and Research, focusing on Holocaust education and commemoration policies, took to speak with me about this project. His insight into the current state of Austrian Holocaust memorialization, and where this project might fit into that landscape, was extremely helpful as I began to think about if or how this story could be related to modern-day Austria and opportunities there.

Finding a publisher who understood what I was doing and was able to support this process was challenging since this is not a traditional story or manuscript. Many thanks to Stephen Kosslyn for his candor and experience-based insights on the publishing process and industry. I have immense gratitude to Liesbeth Heenk and the editorial team at Amsterdam Publishers for taking the final steps, supporting me and this work, and bringing this labor of love out into the world, as they have with so many other important stories for which they provided a unique home.

I am grateful for family who love and support me even when they would not necessarily tell this story themselves. To my parents, Stephanie Wald Hand and Barry Hand, thank you for believing in me and supporting me as long as I can remember. I would not have come so far in this world without you. To my mother, thank you for coming along with me for this ride even when it was odd or uncomfortable and not a path you would have chosen to go down by yourself. I appreciate going through much of this together, and I will always be grateful that you were willing to see where all of this would go and be a part of it, too. To my father, thank you for your support and your humor, even when your grandfather's fighting in the Austro-Hungarian army during World War I did not give you eligibility for Austrian citizenship yourself. To my brother, Eddie Hand, and my sister-in-law, Allyson Gotsell-Hand, I hope this process was also meaningful for you both and continues to open new and exciting doors for you, Wally, and whoever else will come down the line.

To Vicente Flores, my partner in love and life for the past 17 years, thank you for encouraging and inspiring me to be the best and most vibrant version of myself. Thank you so much for everything in the life we have built over all this time. We have grown and changed so much over our years together. I hope we continue to grow and change together. The version of me that you see allows me to push past the doubting voices in my head, the voices that question if what I have to say matters. It does, and this work would not have been possible without you.

To the Maxes – my grandfather and my son – thank you for the light you brought and bring to this world. Thank you for inspiring me, each in your own way. The Jewish tradition of naming children after relatives with long and fruitful lives makes me proud to be able to cycle this name into the world again and see what world this newly grown Max both inherits and makes his own. Eventually, when he reads this book, he will know that he comes from a past that was both complicated and full of love and joy. I hope he is always able to lean toward love and joy, to put vibrancy and a well, fully lived life out into the world.

ABOUT THE AUTHOR

Anne Hand was born in 1985 in New York. Her grandmother was a librarian, and she grew up attached to the power of the written word. Her love of books and the worlds they transported her to have always fueled her desire to make change in the world.

Anne has spent her career blending research, policy, and practice to create social impact across the Americas and beyond. She is a recognized expert in global education and development, frequently publishing on topics related to technology and social impact. She holds a B.Sc. from McGill University and an Ed.M. from Harvard University.

Austrian Again. Reclaiming a Lost Legacy is her first book.

PHOTOS

Waldapfel Family, Vienna, Austria, circa 1913 From left: Leopold Waldapfel, Max Waldapfel, Karoline Waldapfel, Valerie Waldapfel, Irma (Fischer) Waldapfel, Sigmund Waldapfel.

Irma Waldapfel, Vienna, 1929.

Hans Fischer and Ernst Fischer, Ostrava, 1930.

Max Wald and Valerie Wald Ardsley, New York, 1931.

Max Wald, New York City, 1930s.

Irma Waldapfel, Hernals, Vienna, 1935.

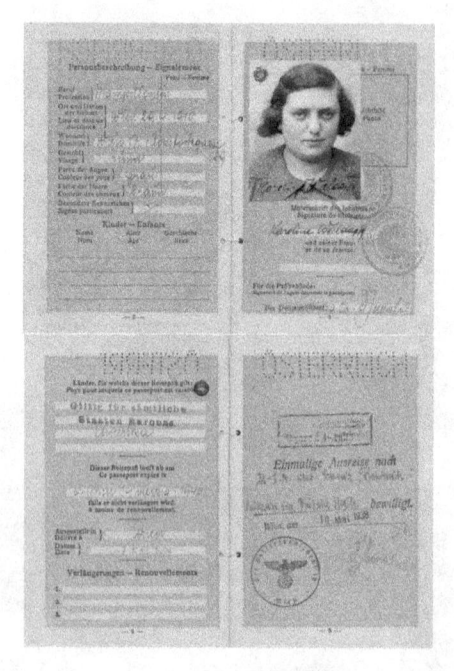

Karoline Waldapfel, Austrian passport, 1938.

Mildred Wald, Irma Wald, and Stephanie Wald Massachusetts, 1952.

Wald-Kressner-Hand Family, New Jersey, 1993 Clockwise from left: David Kressner, Mildred (Wald) Kressner, Arthur Kressner, Barry Hand, Anne Hand, Stephanie (Wald) Hand, Max Wald, Diana Kressner, Pearl (Harris) Wald, Edward Hand.

Anne Hand and Stephanie Hand Austrian Consulate, New York City, 2022.

AMSTERDAM PUBLISHERS HOLOCAUST LIBRARY

The series **Holocaust Survivor Memoirs World War II** consists of the following autobiographies of survivors:

Outcry. Holocaust Memoirs, by Manny Steinberg

Hank Brodt Holocaust Memoirs. A Candle and a Promise, by Deborah Donnelly

The Dead Years. Holocaust Memoirs, by Joseph Schupack

Rescued from the Ashes. The Diary of Leokadia Schmidt, Survivor of the Warsaw Ghetto, by Leokadia Schmidt

My Lvov. Holocaust Memoir of a twelve-year-old Girl, by Janina Hescheles

Remembering Ravensbrück. From Holocaust to Healing, by Natalie Hess

Wolf. A Story of Hate, by Zeev Scheinwald with Ella Scheinwald

Save my Children. An Astonishing Tale of Survival and its Unlikely Hero, by Leon Kleiner with Edwin Stepp

Holocaust Memoirs of a Bergen-Belsen Survivor & Classmate of Anne Frank, by Nanette Blitz Konig

Defiant German - Defiant Jew. A Holocaust Memoir from inside the Third Reich, by Walter Leopold with Les Leopold

In a Land of Forest and Darkness. The Holocaust Story of two Jewish Partisans, by Sara Lustigman Omelinski

Holocaust Memories. Annihilation and Survival in Slovakia, by Paul Davidovits

From Auschwitz with Love. The Inspiring Memoir of Two Sisters' Survival, Devotion and Triumph Told by Manci Grunberger Beran & Ruth Grunberger Mermelstein, by Daniel Seymour

Remetz. Resistance Fighter and Survivor of the Warsaw Ghetto, by Jan Yohay Remetz

My March Through Hell. A Young Girl's Terrifying Journey to Survival, by Halina Kleiner with Edwin Stepp

Roman's Journey, by Roman Halter

Beyond Borders. Escaping the Holocaust and Fighting the Nazis. 1938-1948, by Rudi Haymann

The Engineers. A memoir of survival through World War II in Poland and Hungary, by Henry Reiss

Spark of Hope. An Autobiography, by Luba Wrobel Goldberg

Footnote to History. From Hungary to America. The Memoir of a Holocaust Survivor, by Andrew Laszlo

Farewell Atlantis. Recollections, by Valentīna Freimane

The Courtyard. A memoir, by Benjamin Parket and Alexa Morris

The Mulberry Tree. The story of a life before and after the Holocaust, by Iboja Wandall-Holm

The Boy in the Back. A True Story of Survival in Auschwitz and Mauthausen, as told to Fern Lebo by Jan Blumenstein

Beneath the Lightless Sky. Surviving the Holocaust in the Sewers of Lvov, by Ignacy Chiger

Mendel Run, by Milton H. Schwartz

The series **Holocaust Survivor True Stories**
consists of the following biographies:

Among the Reeds. The true story of how a family survived the Holocaust, by Tammy Bottner

A Holocaust Memoir of Love & Resilience. Mama's Survival from Lithuania to America, by Ettie Zilber

Living among the Dead. My Grandmother's Holocaust Survival Story of Love and Strength, by Adena Bernstein Astrowsky

Heart Songs. A Holocaust Memoir, by Barbara Gilford

Shoes of the Shoah. The Tomorrow of Yesterday, by Dorothy Pierce

Hidden in Berlin. A Holocaust Memoir, by Evelyn Joseph Grossman

Separated Together. The Incredible True WWII Story of Soulmates Stranded an Ocean Apart, by Kenneth P. Price, Ph.D.

The Man Across the River. The incredible story of one man's will to survive the Holocaust, by Zvi Wiesenfeld

If Anyone Calls, Tell Them I Died. A Memoir, by Emanuel (Manu) Rosen

The House on Thrömerstrasse. A Story of Rebirth and Renewal in the Wake of the Holocaust, by Ron Vincent

Dancing with my Father. His hidden past. Her quest for truth. How Nazi Vienna shaped a family's identity, by Jo Sorochinsky

The Story Keeper. Weaving the Threads of Time and Memory - A Memoir, by Fred Feldman

Krisia's Silence. The Girl who was not on Schindler's List, by Ronny Hein

Defying Death on the Danube. A Holocaust Survival Story, by Debbie J. Callahan with Henry Stern

A Doorway to Heroism. A decorated German-Jewish Soldier who became an American Hero, by W. Jack Romberg

The Shoemaker's Son. The Life of a Holocaust Resister, by Laura Beth Bakst

The Redhead of Auschwitz. A True Story, by Nechama Birnbaum

Land of Many Bridges. My Father's Story, by Bela Ruth Samuel Tenenholtz

Creating Beauty from the Abyss. The Amazing Story of Sam Herciger, Auschwitz Survivor and Artist, by Lesley Ann Richardson

On Sunny Days We Sang. A Holocaust Story of Survival and Resilience, by Jeannette Grunhaus de Gelman

Painful Joy. A Holocaust Family Memoir, by Max J. Friedman

I Give You My Heart. A True Story of Courage and Survival, by Wendy Holden

In the Time of Madmen, by Mark A. Prelas

Monsters and Miracles. Horror, Heroes and the Holocaust, by Ira Wesley Kitmacher

Flower of Vlora. Growing up Jewish in Communist Albania, by Anna Kohen

Aftermath: Coming of Age on Three Continents. A Memoir, by Annette Libeskind Berkovits

Not a real Enemy. The True Story of a Hungarian Jewish Man's Fight for Freedom, by Robert Wolf

Zaidy's War. Four Armies, Three Continents, Two Brothers. One Man's Impossible Story of Endurance, by Martin Bodek

The Glassmaker's Son. Looking for the World my Father left behind in Nazi Germany, by Peter Kupfer

The Apprentice of Buchenwald. The True Story of the Teenage Boy Who Sabotaged Hitler's War Machine, by Oren Schneider

Good for a Single Journey, by Helen Joyce

Burying the Ghosts. She escaped Nazi Germany only to have her life torn apart by the woman she saved from the camps: her mother, by Sonia Case

American Wolf. From Nazi Refugee to American Spy. A True Story, by Audrey Birnbaum

Bipolar Refugee. A Saga of Survival and Resilience, by Peter Wiesner

In the Wake of Madness. My Family's Escape from the Nazis, by Bettie Lennett Denny

Before the Beginning and After the End, by Hymie Anisman

I Will Give Them an Everlasting Name. Jacksonville's Stories of the Holocaust, by Samuel Cox

Hiding in Holland. A Resistance Memoir, by Shulamit Reinharz

The Ghosts on the Wall. A Grandson's Memoir of the Holocaust, by Kenneth D. Wald

Thirteen in Auschwitz. My grandmother's fight to stay human, by Lauren Meyerowitz Port

Little Edna's War. The gripping WWII page-turner – a true story of resistance and hope, by Janet Bond Brill PhD

The Jewish Woman Who Fought the Nazis. Bep Schaap-Bedak's life during the Holocaust in Holland, by Eli Schaap

Voices of Resilience. An Anthology of Stories written by Children of Holocaust Survivors, Edited by Deborah (Devora) Ross-Grayman

Dreaming of the River, by Pauline Steinhorn

The series **Jewish Children in the Holocaust** consists of the following autobiographies of Jewish children hidden during WWII in the Netherlands:

Searching for Home. The Impact of WWII on a Hidden Child,
by Joseph Gosler

Sounds from Silence. Reflections of a Child Holocaust Survivor, Psychiatrist and Teacher, by Robert Krell

Sabine's Odyssey. A Hidden Child and her Dutch Rescuers,
by Agnes Schipper

The Journey of a Hidden Child,

by Harry Pila and Robin Black

The series **New Jewish Fiction** consists of the following novels, written by Jewish authors. All novels are set in the time during or after the Holocaust.

The Corset Maker. A Novel, by Annette Libeskind Berkovits

Escaping the Whale. The Holocaust is over. But is it ever over for the next generation? by Ruth Rotkowitz

When the Music Stopped. Willy Rosen's Holocaust, by Casey Hayes

Hands of Gold. One Man's Quest to Find the Silver Lining in Misfortune, by Roni Robbins

The Girl Who Counted Numbers. A Novel, by Roslyn Bernstein

There was a garden in Nuremberg. A Novel, by Navina Michal Clemerson

The Butterfly and the Axe, by Omer Bartov

To Live Another Day. A Novel, by Elizabeth Rosenberg

The Right to Happiness. After all they went through. Stories, by Helen Schary Motro

Five Amber Beads, by Richard Aronowitz

To Love Another Day. A Novel, by Elizabeth Rosenberg

Cursing the Darkness. A Novel about Loss and Recovery, by Joanna Rosenthall

The series **Holocaust Heritage** consists of the following memoirs by 2G:

The Cello Still Sings. A Generational Story of the Holocaust and of the Transformative Power of Music, by Janet Horvath

The Fire and the Bonfire. A Journey into Memory, by Ardyn Halter

The Silk Factory: Finding Threads of My Family's True Holocaust Story, by Michael Hickins

Winter Light. The Memoir of a Child of Holocaust Survivors, by Grace Feuerverger

Out from the Shadows. Growing up with Holocaust Survivor Parents, by Willie Handler

Hidden in Plain Sight. A Family Memoir and the Untold Story of the Holocaust in Serbia, by Julie Brill

The Unspeakable. Breaking my family's silence surrounding the Holocaust, by Nicola Hanefeld

Eighteen for Life. Surviving the Holocaust,

by Helen Schamroth

Four Survivor Grandparents. Run. Rely. Rebuild, by Jonathan Schloss

Austrian Again. Reclaiming a Lost Legacy,

by Anne Hand

Divine Corners, by Michelle Friedman

The series **Holocaust Books for Young Adults** consists of the following novels, based on true stories:

The Boy behind the Door. How Salomon Kool Escaped the Nazis. Inspired by a True Story, by David Tabatsky

Running for Shelter. A True Story, by Suzette Sheft

The Precious Few. An Inspirational Saga of Courage based on True Stories, by David Twain with Art Twain

Dark Shadows Hover, by Jordan Steven Sher

The Sun will Shine Again, by Cynthia Goldstein Monsour

The Memory Place. How My Parents Survived 17 Concentration Camps, by Monica van Rijn

The series **WWII Historical Fiction** consists of the following novels, some of which are based on true stories:

Mendelevski's Box. A Heartwarming and Heartbreaking Jewish Survivor's Story, by Roger Swindells

A Quiet Genocide. The Untold Holocaust of Disabled Children in WWII Germany, by Glenn Bryant

The Knife-Edge Path, by Patrick T. Leahy

Brave Face. The Inspiring WWII Memoir of a Dutch/German Child, by I. Caroline Crocker and Meta A. Evenbly

When We Had Wings. The Gripping Story of an Orphan in Janusz Korczak's Orphanage. A Historical Novel, by Tami Shem-Tov

Jacob's Courage. Romance and Survival amidst the Horrors of War, by Charles S. Weinblatt

A Semblance of Justice. Based on true Holocaust experiences, by Wolf Holles

Under the Pink Triangle. Where forbidden love meets unspeakable evil, by Katie Moore